CHINESE SHAR-PEI
KW-156

Photography: Isabelle Francais, Bruce K. Harkins, Palmer Photos, Robert Pearcy, and Skibinski Photography.

Drawings by *Scott Boldt, Richard Crammer, Richard Davis, Andrew Prendimano, John Quinn, and Alexandra Suchenka.*

Front endpapers: *Uniqueness and personality perhaps explain the extraordinary upsurge of popularity for the Chinese Shar-pei in recent times. These dogs are owned by Gerald and Patricia Brown.*

Title page: *Affectionate and expressive, the Chinese Shar-pei makes a wonderfully pleasing and endearing companion. Owners, Gerald and Patricia Brown.*

Distributed in the UNITED STATES by T.F.H. Publications, Inc., One T.F.H. Plaza, Neptune City, NJ 07753; in CANADA to the Pet Trade by H & L Pet Supplies Inc., 27 Kingston Crescent, Kitchener, Ontario N2B 2T6; Rolf C. Hagen Ltd., 3225 Sartelon Street, Montreal 382 Quebec; in CANADA to the Book Trade by Macmillan of Canada (A Division of Canada Publishing Corporation), 164 Commander Boulevard, Agincourt, Ontario M1S 3C7; in ENGLAND by T.F.H. Publications Limited, Cliveden House/Priors Way/Bray, Maidenhead, Berkshire SL6 2HP, England; in AUSTRALIA AND THE SOUTH PACIFIC by T.F.H. (Australia) Pty. Ltd., Box 149, Brookvale 2100 N.S.W., Australia; in NEW ZEALAND by Ross Haines & Son, Ltd., 18 Monmouth Street, Grey Lynn, Auckland 2, New Zealand; in SINGAPORE AND MALAYSIA by MPH Distributors (S) Pte., Ltd., 601 Sims Drive, #03/07/21, Singapore 1438; in the PHILIPPINES by Bio-Research, 5 Lippay Street, San Lorenzo Village, Makati Rizal; in SOUTH AFRICA by Multipet Pty. Ltd., 30 Turners Avenue, Durban 4001. Published by T.F.H. Publications, Inc. Manufactured in the United States of America by T.F.H. Publications, Inc.

CHINESE SHAR-PEI

ANNA KATHERINE NICHOLAS

Much indebted to the efforts of a handful of Shar-pei enthusiasts devoted to saving the breed from destruction,
owners today are ever so fortunate to have these delightful and dignified fellows to share their homes and
lives with. K. Derrick Paulus is the owner of these two
Shar-pei.

Contents

Origin and Early History of the Chinese Shar-Pei

The Chinese Shar-Pei is one of the earliest breeds of dog known to man, although not always by that name. The dogs considered the progenitors of this modern breed were in existence as long ago as some twenty centuries, having been a definite type since the Han Dynasty (ca. 220 AD). Thus, in common with most Chinese breeds, its roots are deeply buried in the sands of time.

That these dogs were held in high esteem is undeniable, for very many artifacts featuring these hippopotamus-resembling canines have been found by archeologists who have frequently referred to them as "Tomb Dogs." The resemblance in this statuary is quite clear, including the unique blunt muzzle and other facial characteristics which set these dogs apart from others. We know that at least one statue of a "Tomb Dog" has been, and quite probably still is, displayed in the Avery Brundage Collection at the Asian Art Museum, San Francisco, California.

The most widely expressed belief regarding the origin of these dogs is that they were native to the South China Sea area; more specifically, a small town named Dah Let in the province of Kwong Tung. Another theory is that the dogs actually originated in Tibet or in northern China and were known there prior to their appearance in Dah Let. Who is to say for certain after all these years?

The forebears of the Shar-Pei have been described as being a great deal larger than the dogs we now know of this breed, weighing on the average about 165 pounds.

Our modern Shar-Pei has inherited many of the original dog's characteristics. Standing 18 to 20 inches at the withers, this unique dog, unlike any other under the canine sun, combines all the distinctive hippo-like features which set him apart from all other types of dog. China has developed some of dogdom's most unique breeds, a tradition in which the Shar-Pei definitely plays his part!

As a breed, the Shar-Pei started out as a working farm dog. He was owned by the Chinese peasant to whom he was extremely useful. Generations of Shar-Pei have distinguished themselves as guard dogs, herders, and companion dogs. Then as now, they were loyal, reliable, alert, and intelligent— exactly what the peasants, many living in isolated areas, needed for the protection of themselves and their property.

Facing page: Exotic and extraordinary, the Chinese Shar-pei expands the Orient's already existing list of exceptional breeds. Owners, Gerald and Patricia Brown.

"SERVICE DOG" OR "FIGHTING DOG"

So well did the early Shar-Pei ancestors fulfill their duties that they became known as "Service Dogs." For hundreds of years they were also known as "Chinese Fighting Dogs." It has been explained, however, that this is not truly an accurate description of the breeds employment, for although he was occasionally used for pit fighting, he was more commonly used for service-oriented functions.

The early Shar-Pei has been especially praised for his herding talents, and the success he enjoyed hunting game in China.

As "Fighting Dogs," these early ancestors of the Shar-Pei evidently were not overly successful against other breeds. The principal interest in

This handsome dog is Down-Homes China Souel who was imported from Matgo Law in Hong Kong by Ernest Albright of Pleasant Hill, California.

developing this aspect of their personality came about in Canton, a city close to Dah Let. Here the sporting and gambling elements were attached. With little in those days to be offered for amusement, some of the gamblers turned their attention towards developing the fighting talents of the dogs. The poverty-stricken peasants of the area were ready and willing to participate in whatever might be available to help put a bit of gold in their pockets.

The Chinese Fighting Dogs were well-equipped in several ways for the activity—the same features which made them successful hunters were also helpful in this capacity. The looseness of skin which enabled a dog, even with his skin in the grip of an opponent's teeth, to twist and attack the other animal served as a protection to his internal organs, creating a nearly impenetrable buffer from his attacker's grip.

The principal distinguishing characteristic of the Shar-Pei *is* his coat; but not its *looseness* so much as its *texture* for which the breed was named, "Shar-Pei" meaning "sand skin." This coat is extremely rough and bristly in texture, most uncomfortable in the mouth of another canine or wild animal.

His small, deep-set eyes make the Shar-Pei less vulnerable to eye injuries; similarly, his tiny ears present little area for painful injury.

Standing proud at three months of age, this is Tail's End Kinni Kinnick, owned by Ann Coleman of Tail's End Shar-Pei.

The formation of the teeth make them a powerful weapon, the curved canine scimitars, once clasped on an opponent, are extremely difficult to escape. For generations now the Shar-Pei has been bred for "scissors" bite as have the majority of dog breeds.

The story goes that eventually the gamblers "discovered" the Western fighting dogs which surpassed the Chinese dogs in weight and proficiency. It has been said that, although physically well-equipped for combat, the Shar-Pei did not appear to have much heart to fight, being basically friendly and amiable. In reality, it took intensive training and the help of stimulants to persuade him to fight in the pits. Actually, the Shar-Pei was much happier at home fending off intruders on his master's property than matching power and wits with other dogs in a pit.

With less interest in the fighting dog lifestyle, these fine animals returned to their original roles of farm and family dog. Actually it was only a comparitively small number of them who had been involved in the pits, as many peasants who relied on them for protection were appalled to see their reliable pets and protectors killed or maimed in this manner.

Interestingly, although we have seen references to Chinese Fighting Dogs upon occasion, as of 1960 (and we doubt that they have since done so), no official recognition of them as a breed has been included in the registry of any governing kennel club or leading kennel council.

It is difficult to comprehend, as one considers the escalating rise in popularity of the Chinese Shar-Pei and of Shar-Pei owners and fanciers, that less than two decades ago, during the late 1960s, the number of Shar-Pei had become so alarmingly small that complete extinction seemed both imminent and unavoidable. *The Guinness Book of World Records* noted this fact by listing the Shar-Pei as "the rarest breed of dog in the world," a dubious honor considering what the

Offspring of two wondrously celestial Champion parents, this is Alpha Devil's Promenade at three months of age. He is owned by Ann Coleman, Tail's End Shar-Pei.

possible outcome might have been. For without question, had that trend been permitted to continue, there would by now be no Shar-Pei left for the animal lovers of the world to enjoy.

THE PEOPLE'S REPUBLIC OF CHINA

The Communist Party takeover of China created a catastrophic situation for all dogs there. The Communistic viewpoint precludes the "wasting of food" on dogs; thus levied heavy taxation on the ownership of even one. Taxation was periodically increased until, by the late 1940s, there was hardly a dog left to be seen in

China. This definitely hit the poverty-stricken peasants hard. The maintaining of a dog had now become a major expenditure, it took hardly any time at all to reduce the numbers of Shar-Pei to practically zero. It seemed like the beginning of the end for the breed, the first step down the road of the Shar-Pei's trip into extinction.

THE CONTRIBUTION OF MATGO LAW

Having observed the outcome of the Communist Party's rule in China on the nation's dog population, a great friend of the Shar-Pei, Matgo Law, feared that Hong Kong might one day also be taken over by the People's Republic. To him it was unthinkable that a similar destruction of dogs might be repeated in Hong Kong. Determined to protect and assure a future for his beloved breed, a man who did not believe in sitting passively and watching such horrors take place, Law decided that prompt and decisive action on behalf of the Shar-Pei must take place.

Having seen at one time a magazine article featuring the names of endangered breeds, Law wrote a letter to an American magazine in hopes of what might develop. This letter extolled the qualities of the Shar-Pei, included a picture or two, and asked if any American dog lovers might be willing to help save a breed. The letter went out to the magazine with faint hope, as Mr. Law was far from confident that there would be any reply whatsoever. How elated he must have been when the response added up to more than 200 people not only willing but eager to pick up the challenge

An exceptional puppy at the House of Sheng Li. Owner-bred by R.L. and Vicky Teshera.

and rescue the Shar-Pei from potential destruction.

Consequently, the amount of Shar-Pei breeding in Hong Kong was not sufficient to even make a dent in the number of orders. However, there was some breeding stock in Hong Kong (one would imagine that some of the Chinese owners may have gotten some of their dogs into the hands of the Hong Kong breeders when the new tax laws tightened on dog owners on the Communist mainland). There were other breeders, we are sure, in addition to Mr. Law in Hong Kong.

Patiently and/or pensively, Astra peers into the camera. Owners, R.L. and Vicky Teshera.

EVOLUTION OF THE PRESENT-DAY SHAR-PEI

We understand that, as of the present time, there still are a few Shar-Pei dogs of the original Chinese lines left in China. It has been said that the modern Shar-Pei, as we know the breed today, is not descended purely from Chinese stock, but that somewhere along the line an outcross or two was introduced. The breeds included most frequently as probabilities are the Chow Chow, the Bull Mastiff, the Boxer, and the Bull Terrier. Simply observing the breeds, one can note similarities between the Shar-Pei and the Chow Chow, and even members of the Mastiff family (scaled down to a far smaller size). There are decidedly mutual characteristics between Chows and the Shar-Pei; and between Shar-Pei and certain of the Mastiffs. Where this crossbreeding might have occurred is difficult to say.

Joseph Chan, who was born and raised in Macau, lives in California but still spend time in China. Mr. Chan, writing for the American magazine *Dog World,* tells his readers that he keeps in constant touch with the remaining Shar-Pei owners in Macau. His feeling, as stated in the article and to me in conversation, is that, "Due to the political climate from the early 1950 period through the mid-1960s, the only place for Hong Kong people to obtain Shar-Pei was from Macau. At that time in Hong Kong, Shar-Pei were non-existent". Mr. Chan mentions that there are experienced breeders in the United States who have suspected that the Shar-Pei is a modified breed, and his comment on this is "that they were right all along. This mixed breed consists of the Chinese Shar-Pei bred to

Sound and handsome, this beautifully balanced Shar-pei is owned by Dianne Barlow. The heavy bone and flawless head are marks of his exquisite type. He is Ch. Alpha Artic Gorilla Remington.

the Bull Mastiff, Chow Chow, Bulldog, Boxer, and Bull Terrier."

We will leave it to the reader to reach his own decision on this matter. The writer's personal comment is that if such *did* take place, it is a rather common practice in establishing and improving a breed; and I daresay that there are very few breeds of dog who have come down through the ages without an outcross or two somewhere along the way to "set" certain characteristics, to improve others, to establish size, etc.

THE CHINESE STANDARD FOR THE SHAR-PEI

Mr. Chan has given us permission to use parts of his translated interpretation of the true Chinese Standard for Shar-Pei, which is especially intriguing. The Chinese custom is to refer to the most commonly known similar shape or form to describe each part of the dog. Also, the first eight parts of the Chinese Standard are given in sequence which when recited in Cantonese are in the form of a poem.

What the Chinese standard, as translated, calls for is as follows:

WU-LO HEAD—The shape of a Wu-Lo melon, (like a pear). Heavy and round at the bottom (skull); tapered at the top (muzzle).

CLAM SHELL EAR—Ear similar to small clam shell. Thick and

small.

BUTTERFLY NOSE—There is a cookie in Guangzhou, China, called "butterfly" of similar appearance to a front view of the dog's nose, with a very wide nostril. The dog's nose should be big (wide) and blunt.

PAE PAH LEGS—The Pae Pah is a musical instrument shaped like a ham. The hind legs should be thick, muscled, and straight without any angulation.

SHRIMP BACK—Back is strong and flexible, no dip behind withers. The croup is flat, not steep or round. In normal posture, the back is slightly arched, almost straight. The difference between the roach back and the shrimp back is that the shrimp back is flexible while the roach back remains permanent.

IRON-WIRE TAIL—Tail should

be stiff and thin at the base like a piece of cable, high set on the back. Preferably the tail makes a tight round curl; so tight that a small hole, like a coin, forms in the center of this tail. To the Chinese, the correct tail is of great importance.

GRANDMA FACE—Describes the facial wrinkling, just a little like "Granny's." The face should not be overly wrinkled.

IRON PELLET TONGUE—Bluish black color like an iron pellet. In China, a "flowered" tongue is acceptable.

WATER BUFFALO NECK—Strong and of medium length, with a small amount of dewlap, like a water buffalo.

WUN FISH BODY—A common fish in Kwong Tung Province describes body that is, like this fish, not too round nor too flat in rib cage. Dry and firm. Skin tight without wrinkles except in the withers area. When skin is grabbed and pulled away from body it should be extremely loose.

FACING SKY ANUS—Tail set so high on back that the anus protrudes slightly and faces upwards. Has noticeable rim.

HORSE'S REAR END—Broad, muscular, well-developed, like that of a horse.

Ch. Commodity of Tail's End is owned by Ann Coleman. She is a cream female of noteworthy type who is both a Group winner and a Best of Breed winner.

These three horsecoat puppies of Fingertail Charmin have certainly cornered the market on irresistibility and charm. They are owned by Jo Ann Webster.

DRAGON LEG—Front legs wide-spaced to side of body forming very wide chest.

GARLIC FEET—Thick, firm, well-knuckled. Resembles garlic bulb with toes forming the garlic cloves.

MOTHER FROG MOUTH—Muzzle short, wide, tapered to blunt wedge triangle. When opened, corners of mouth wider than placement of eyes.

ROOF TILE MOUTH—Longer than the preferred Mother Frog Mouth. Muzzle strong, round in shape. Resembles Chinese Roof Tile.

IRON TOENAIL—Bluish black.

RUSTY BLACK—Color of a black dog's coat which should be dull, not shiny, with tips of hair ending in reddish brown, like rust.

FIVE (POINT) RED—This does not refer to coat color, but to five areas of the body which may be red or pink on dogs of diluted pigmentation (meaning coat colors of red, light fawn, cream, or white). These parts are the nose, eye rims, tongue, toenails, and anus.

In China, the two preferred coat colors would appear to be rusty black and dark fawn.

Development of the Shar-Pei Outside China

THE SHAR-PEI IN THE UNITED STATES

A warm, highly enthusiastic reception greeted the Shar-Pei as they began arriving from Hong Kong into the United States. The moment dog lovers saw them they wanted to own one; and obviously the supply was limited, leaving many would-be owners waiting patiently for their puppies to be born.

America loves the new, the different, and the chance to be in on the start of something important. The Shar-Pei covers all these categories. Plus very definitely it can be said of this breed "that to know one is to love one" as only a short acquaintance is needed before one starts to appreciate the intelligence and marvelous disposition of these dogs.

What a fortunate day it was for the future of this breed when Mr. and Mrs. Ernest Albright of California became attracted to it. The Albrights had partially retired at just about the time Matgo Law's letter describing the plight of the Shar-Pei appeared in the American press. Additionally, they had been seriously considering involving themselves in dog breeding but had not decided on a particular breed.

The news of the Shar-Pei appealed to them instantly and they decided to take on this project.

Mr. Albright started to wage a "Shar-Pei Publicity Campaign" that turned out to be enormously successful. His dogs were shown and discussed on television and in the press. Additionally, he spent untold hours in discussion of the breed with interested parties, sharing his knowledge and understanding of the breed. Mr. Albright's efforts for the breed in the U.S. and Mr. Law's work in Hong Kong both were entirely successful and blossomed within an amazingly short length of time. Prior to the breed's actually arriving in America, their popularity mushroomed as many

A pup of promise, this is Tzo Tzo's Mamie of Tail's End photographed at two and a half months of age. She is owned by Ann Coleman.

Lounging away the afternoon, here lies House of Treasures Oprah with House of Treasures Mason—although shown here with less flurry and chatter than usual, they are ofttimes filled with uninterruptable activity. Bred by Barbara and Gary Roche.

visitors to Hong Kong who saw them either returned with a puppy or ordered one. Among these were numerous prominent U.S. judges and other visitors to the Orient. The first this writer knew of them was through the John Pattersons, noted Basset Hound breeders and popular multiple breed judges, who brought back pictures of the new dogs that they were going to breed. These dogs brought the Pattersons great pleasure, and they have continued to be favorites of the family.

The Albrights, whose dogs are known as the Ho Wun Chinese Shar-Pei, received their first two during the early 1970s. Their breeding program took off in 1974. The Board of Governors of the Shar Pei Club of America have recently passed a Resolution that Albright be recognized as an Honorary Lifetime Director and President Emeritus as an expression of thanks, respect, and admiration of a job well-done. Albright had previously served as founder member, president, and director of the Shar Pei Club of America from 1974 to 1981.

ALBRIGHT'S DISTINGUISHED SHAR-PEI

Albright's famous dogs are the handsome stud dog Chin China Souel, who was born in Hong Kong from Chinese stock. Mui-Chu helped promote the breed's popularity when she was featured on the cover of *Popular Dogs*

Magazine in 1973. Ming Yun, from the first Albright homebred litter, became a quite well-known television star by her appearance with David Frost, Garry Moore, and on such widely viewed programs as *To Tell The Truth* and *Good Morning, America.* Shima, another Albright dog, was a star for a Japanese movie on television in 1979. Ting helped to publicize the breed in Canada by making guest appearances at a school exhibit, the large and prestigious Metropolitan Kennel Club Dog Show, and as the subject of numerous newspaper stories. Fawn appeared in 600 newspapers and magazines and at Canada's Metropolitan Kennel Club in 1978. Tibet who did stunts for Johnny Carson on *The Tonight Show* in March, 1979, was invited by Betty White to her show and received a wide range of press coverage. On reviewing all this, one must comment that Mr. Albright really does know how to run an advertising campaign; and that such wide coverage must have made every person in the North American countries realize that the Shar-Pei's future was to be a bright one!

The Chinese Shar-Pei Club of America is the National Parent Specialty for the breed. It is the responsibility of this organization to keep the registry until the breed is admitted into the American Kennel Club Stud Book, at which point the records are turned over to A.K.C. The Shar-Pei Club also holds specialty shows, match shows, and other competitive events for the breed. They award the title "Champion" to any Shar-Pei having acquired the requisite number of points to earn this distinction. All of the dogs pictured in this book who bear titles have gained them from the CSPCA.

THE ROAD TO TAKE

There will be new worlds to conquer when the Shar-Pei receives its own breed classification as being fully recognized by the American Kennel Club. The first breakthrough came in the admittance of the breed to the Miscellaneous Class at dog shows. This became effective on May 4, 1988.

The following step will be admittance to the Stud Book when the required number of Shar-Pei have been CSPCA-registered. We understand that now about 40,000 Shar-Pei are already listed in the registry. And finally comes the breed's own classification as an American Kennel Club-recognized breed at dog shows. This is exciting to contemplate as many breeders are truly producing dogs of tremendous quality.

A gentleman deserving high praise from the Shar-Pei fancy is William W. Morison, who has been the registrar for the Chinese Shar-Pei Club of America since 1978 and was the chairman of

Owned by Steve Peloso, this is House of Treasures Mason, a remarkable example of a fawn horse coat male.

committee that negotiated the consolidation of the two existing Shar-Pei clubs. As further proof of his dedication to the breed, he consented to take on the added responsibility of becoming membership secretary in 1984. Mr. Morison is a native Californian having been born and raised in the Bay area.

Throughout the United States, there are many affiliated clubs to the National, all with busy, ambitious program schedules. Fun, education, and good exposure of the breed are among the purposes of these organizations. These clubs hold specialty shows (sometimes two annually) and support the breed at rare breed shows in which the Shar-Pei has done quite spectacularly.

In the East, the Northeastern Shar-Pei Club is an especially involved organization, and we believe is the first for the breed whose members have supported temperament tests for their dogs, a number of whom have earned TT degrees.

Those wishing to inquire about a Shar-Pei club in their area or any other aspect of the breed and its ownership should contact the Shar-Pei Club of America, Inc., at 9705 East 80th Street, Raytown, Missouri. Also, information can be sought from the Shar-Pei Club of America's Registry address, 55 Oak Court, Danville, California, 94526.

Development Outside China

A thorough study of the Standard of Perfection as drawn up by the Chinese Shar-Pei Club of America, effective May, 1988, is most helpful, as familiarity with this detailed description will help familiarize the reader with the desirable and the less desirable physical characteristics of this breed.

SHAR-PEI AROUND THE WORLD

Although there could be but little argument that Hong Kong and the United States have been the seats of the greatest activity in the Shar-Pei world recently, we are pleased to know that the breed is being popularized and working towards official recognition in other important strongholds of dog lovers, too.

Australia, for example, has a nucleus of people "into" the Shar-Pei, working hard to benefit the breed with official recognition being their desired goal.

Canada was rather in the "fringe benefit" area of Mr. Albright's publicity campaign in the states. Much that was written about the breed in the U.S. was read and studied there; the dogs were displayed at important Canadian dog shows, and the day may not be too far off when Shar-Pei fanciers shall receive word from the Canadian Kennel Club that official recognition is nearing.

We have heard little on the subject of the Shar-Pei in Great Britain so far: but we feel safely assured that there is interest in that country, too.

Tibet, Taiwan, and the

This red brush male is Fingertail Yunny. The Shar-pei is loved for his mellow disposition and gentle manner. Owner, Jo Ann Webster.

Peering prophetically over the formidable vastness of the outside world, this is Cra-Jack's H.O.T. Sugar at three months. A cream dilute from House of Treasures.

Philippines have been mentioned as strongholds which the breed enjoys.

But there is still a long way to go! Let us not forget that the breed only first started to attract attention in the early 1970s. We expect big things for the Shar-Pei and its friends in the future. Wait and see!

AMERICAN STANDARD

The following is the American Standard for the Chinese Shar-Pei by the Chinese Shar-Pei Club of America, Inc.

GENERAL APPEARANCE—An alert, dignified, active, compact dog of medium size and substance, square in profile, close-coupled, the well-proportioned head slightly but not overly large for the body. The short, harsh coat, the loose skin covering the head and body, the small ears, the "hippopotamus" muzzle shape and the high set tail impart to the Shar-Pei a unique look peculiar to him alone. The loose skin and wrinkles covering the head, neck and body are superabundant in puppies but these features may be limited to the head, neck and withers in the adult.

HEAD—Large, slightly but not overly, proudly carried and covered with profuse wrinkles on the forehead continuing into side wrinkles framing the face. SKULL—Flat and broad, the stop moderately defined, the length from nose to stop is approximately the same as from stop to occiput. MUZZLE—One of the distinctive

With dazzling promise, this is Remington's Arctic Stardust owned by Dianne Barlow.

features of the breed. It is broad and full with no suggestion of snipiness. The lips and top of muzzle are well padded and may cause a slight bulge at the base of the nose. NOSE—Large and wide and darkly pigmented, preferably black but any color nose conforming to the general coat color of the dog is acceptable. In dilute colors, the preferred nose is self-colored. Darkly pigmented cream Shar-Pei may have some light pigment either in the center of their noses or on their entire nose. TEETH—Strong, meeting in a scissors bite. Deviation from a scissor bite is a major fault. EYES—Dark, small, almond-shaped and sunken, displaying a scowling expression. In the dilute-colored dogs, the eye color may be lighter. EARS—Extremely small, rather thick, equilateral triangles in shape, slightly rounded at the tips, edges of the ear may curl. Ears lie flat against the head, are set wide apart and forward on the skull, pointing toward the eyes. The ears have the ability to move. Pricked ears are a disqualification. TONGUE, ROOF OF MOUTH, GUMS AND FLEWS—Solid bluish black is preferred in all coat colors except in dilute colors, which have a solid lavender pigmentation. A spotted tongue is a major fault. A solid pink tongue is a disqualification. (Tongue colors may lighten due to heat stress; care must be taken not to confuse dilute pigmentation with a pink tongue).

BODY—Proportion: The height

Head study of Ch. Meiting Sheng Li of the House of Sheng Li. Owners, R.L. and Vicky Teshera.

of the Shar-Pei from the ground to the withers is approximately equal to the length from the point of breastbone to the point of rump. NECK—Medium length, full and set well into the shoulders. There are moderate to heavy folds of loose skin and abundant dewlap about the neck and throat.

BACK—Short and close-coupled, the topline dips slightly behind the withers, slightly rising over the short, broad loin. CHEST—Broad and deep with the brisket extending to the elbow and rising slightly under the loin. CROUP—Flat, with the base of the tail set extremely high, clearly exposing an uptilted anus. TAIL—The high set tail is a characteristic feature of the Shar-Pei. The tail is thick and round at the base, tapering to a fine point and curling over or to either side of the back. The absence of a complete tail is a disqualification.

FOREQUARTERS—Shoulders: Muscular, well-laid back and sloping. Forelegs: When viewed from the front, straight, moderately spaced, with elbows close to the body. When viewed from the side, the forelegs are straight, the pasterns are strong and flexible. The bone is substantial but never heavy and is of moderate length. FEET—Moderate in size, compact, and firmly set, not splayed. Removal of front dewclaws is optional.

HINDQUARTERS—Muscular, strong, and moderately angulated. The metatarsi (hocks) are short, perpendicular to the ground, and parallel to each other when viewed from the rear. Hind dewclaws must be removed.

COAT—The extremely harsh coat is one of the distinguishing features of the breed. The coat is absolutely straight and offstanding on the main trunk of the body but generally lies somewhat flatter on the limbs. The coat appears healthy without being shiny or lustrous. Acceptable coat lengths may range from the extremely short "horse coat" up to the "brush coat," not to exceed one inch in length at the withers. A soft coat, a wavy coat, a coat in excess of 1 inch in length at the withers, or a coat that has been trimmed is a major fault. The

Shar-Pei is shown in its natural state.

COLOR—Only solid colors are acceptable. A solid-colored dog may have shading, primarily darker down the back and on the ears. The shading must be variations of the same body color (except in sables) and may include darker hairs throughout the coat. The following colors are disqualifying faults: albino, brindle, parti-color (patches), spotted (spots, ticked, roaning), and a tan-pointed pattern (typical black and tan or saddled).

GAIT—The movement of the Shar-Pei is to be judged at a trot. The gait is free and balanced with the feet tending to converge on a center line of gravity when the dog moves at a vigorous trot. The gait combines good forward reach and a strong drive in the hindquarters. Proper movement is essential.

SIZE—The preferred height is 18 to 20 inches at the withers. The preferred weight is 40 to 55 pounds. The dog is usually larger and more square-bodied than the bitch but both appear well proportioned.

TEMPERAMENT—Regal, alert, intelligent, dignified, lordly, scowling, sober, and snobbish; essentially independent and somewhat standoffish with strangers, but extreme in his devotion to his family. The Shar-Pei stands firmly on the ground with a calm, confident stature.

A champion at eight months of age, this is Ch. Meiting Sheng Li—his five-point major wins included among them Best of Breed. He is owned by R.L. and Vicky Teshera.

So many exciting things have happened for the Shar-Pei in America, including its entry into the American Kennel Club in 1992. Few breeds have as many books to boast about, and the reader is well-advised to consult: *The Shar-Pei* (PS-818), *The World of the Chinese Shar-Pei* (TS-176), and *The Book of the Shar-Pei* (TS-150). Each of these authoritative texts also features hundreds of photographs in color and illustrates the breed standard and various types of Shar-Pei which the reader will find helpful.

HONG KONG STANDARD

In addition to the Chinese and American Standards for the Shar-Pei, there also exists the Hong Kong Standard which is somewhat different. The writer believes you will find the color qualifications of the Hong Kong Standard most fascinating reading as they are more specific than the American Standard (A.K.C.—1988). This standard was translated by Matgo Law.

COLOR—Whole colors—black,

red, deep fawn, light fawn, and cream frequently shaded, (the underpart of tail and back of thighs of a lighter color) but not in patches or parti-colored. This is what the Standard says about colors: "The Shar-Pei should always be a solid color, never parti-colored. Shadings in the blacks and fawns are very common and not indicative of parti-colors. Parti-colors, brindle and black and tans should definitely be penalized and certainly not used in breeding programme." Matgo S.H. Law. March 1980.

Black: Often shaded; nose black, born black; quite easily turn to a rusted-grey color in long exposure to sunshine.

Fawn: Deeper or lighter shade of cinnamon (in American Chow's language); often shaded; nose black; is born flesh-color and turns black in about a week's time. Most common color.

Red: Also shaded, but not so distinctive as blacks or fawns; nose black; deep red color is not common.

Cream: Shaded; fawn ears and always associated with brick-colored nose with black rim (this is why this color should be deep brown and tongue color should be completely blue-black, as blue-black as the blacks and fawns.

Dilute: Theoretically cream is a dilute color but the writer tried to distinguish the following described color variety from the 'creams' and termed it 'dilute.' The coat color is a deeper tone of reddish cream; the color of 'hot cream' in the language of Persian Cat breeders. The nose color is lighter brick-colored (lighter than the creams) without dark pigment around the rim. Eye color is usually lighter and the main difference is the tongue color—a shade of overall light-purple instead of solid blue-black. If the overall color pattern is not diluted to an excessive degree, this color is acceptable.

Rust: An overall rusty-grey (not a seasonal rusted-black color and much lighter overall color than the former); the intermixture of black and fawn hairs; shaded, darker along the top of the back, fawn-rusty on legs; the overall appearance of a whole color effect is maintained and no suggestion of distinctive border between darker and lighter color regions. Nose black.

Chocolate: A whole chocolate color with a chocolate nose and yellowish eyes; tongue color is light-purple; it is whole colored, therefore, acceptable. The writer has so far seen only one of this color, born from both black parents.

Except those specially mentioned, the tongue color of all these varieties should be completely blue-black. The stronger and deeper pigments being favored.

His wistful expression tainted by a subdued complacency makes the Chinese Shar-pei a most intriguing animal. Owners, Gerald and Patricia Brown.

Character, Personality and Temperament

Almost certainly it was the strangeness of his appearance that first attracted your attention to the Shar-Pei. A dog so different is immediately eye-catching, leading the onlooker to want to learn more about the breed.

It takes only a very short period of acquaintance before you become enthralled with the Shar-Pei's many splendid qualities, and to find that the unique physical characteristics are actually only the tip of the iceberg where the merits of a Shar-Pei are concerned.

Shar-Pei owners with speed and efficiency will explain to you in detail that this is the breed of the future. They reveal that dogs are delightful in temperament, and that once you have owned one, you never again will be satisfied with any other breed. An intelligent dog, he is of reliable and even disposition, adoring of his family and friends. With strangers possible initial aloofness quickly becomes a friendly wag. His alertness makes him a competent watchdog. He is playful and comical in his antics, thus a source of amusement and cheer.

Devoted to home and family, Shar-Pei are affectionate to the entire family rather than just selecting one person on whom to shower affection. They get on well with children, and are not hard to handle (if the introductions are properly made) with other pets in the household.

Shar-Pei owners have commented that their dogs are close to humans in their reactions and understanding; they are quiet and non-destructive. That they do not have the urge to wander far afield is another asset. However, this does not mean that they should be permitted to wander on their own. Furthermore, an obviously valuable and exotic dog is in constant peril of being stolen for profit.

Shar-Pei fanciers are zealous in protecting the friendliness and good disposition of their dogs. To this end, all puppies are "socialized" from earliest puppyhood, played with, petted, and loved. It is important to the future self-confidence and disposition of any dog that he feel secure and loved and that his natural inclination towards a happy association with the world be encouraged throughout his growing up period.

POTENTIAL MEDICAL PROBLEMS OF THE SHAR-PEI

The ownership of a Shar-Pei, as is the case with any breed of dog, should never be undertaken without a sense of responsibility. It is quite easy to be intrigued by and fall in love with almost any puppy. But when bringing one home, it should be remembered that this is a commitment for the duration of the puppy's hopefully long lifetime. Also, in the case of the Shar-Pei, it is a comparative

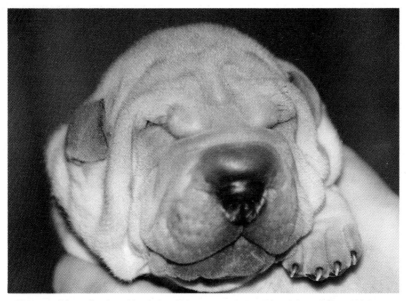

The condition affecting this puppy is known as entropion—it is a defect which requires serious attention by a vet or an experienced breeder. The puppy in this photo belongs to Jo Ann Webster who is one such breeder who has successfully performed the "tacking" procedure on her own.

"new breed" and consequently brings with it some problems which have not yet been completely solved.

Hip dysplasia is a serious condition of which you must be aware. If you are at all planning to use your Shar-Pei as a stud dog or a brood bitch, it is a necessity that you deal with a breeder who is involved with an x-ray program to ascertain the status of the dog you are getting in this regard.

Entropion is a condition in which the edges of the eyelids roll inward, thus bringing the lashes into contact with the eyeball. If left uncorrected, the constant irritation of the lashes rubbing on the eyeball becomes both uncomfortable and dangerous to the eye; thus a simple operation of "tacking" the eyelids should be performed. Some long-time breeders are able to perform this "tacking" themselves. But I strongly advise that it be attended to promptly by a *veterinarian,* and given attention even if the puppy is only a few weeks old. Neglect of this condition can lead to an eye ulcer with the possible loss of the eye to follow. Be on the watch for this with any Shar-Pei you purchase.

There is also a situation involving some Shar-Pei's mouths.

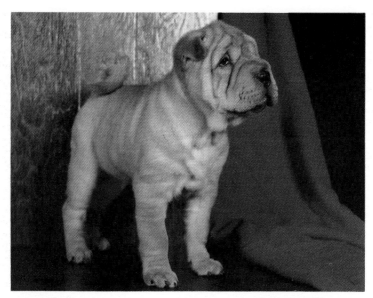

An excellent example of how a future champion appears at eight weeks of age! This is Ch. Hillie's Roisin-Rua Gung Ho (Rosie) owned by Alice Lawler.

In this case the lower lip of the dog has a tendency to roll in over the teeth of the lower jaw, making eating difficult and in severe cases requiring surgical attention.

Another problem area is the breed's tendency toward skin trouble which is certainly not illogical when one considers the number of wrinkles the dogs have. Many breeders have been working on this and have found that mange is *not* involved, as has sometimes been rumored. They believe that it is caused by an allergy to certain foods. Several breeders have expressed an opinion on this, and the concensus is that foods with cornmeal and those with beet sweetening should be avoided. As with human allergies, it can sometimes take a bit of "doing" to track down the culprit. But canine nutritionists have been at work, and you can get the latest "findings" from your veterinarian or an experienced breeder. Again, the breed has not been established for that long and there is still much to learn. Fortunately, breeders are working their hardest to eliminate these problems and will undoubtedly do so in relatively few generations.

Selecting Your Dog

Now that you have decided which dog breed suits your needs, your lifestyle, and your own temperament, there will be much to consider before you make your final purchase. Buying a puppy on impulse may only cause heartbreak later on; it makes better sense to put some real thought into your canine investment, especially since it is likely that he will share many happy years with you. Which individual will you choose as your adoring companion? Ask yourself some questions as you analyze your needs and preferences for a dog, read all that you can about your particular breed, and visit as many dog shows as possible. At the shows you will be surrounded by people who can give you all the details about the breed you are interested in buying. Decide if you want a household pet, a dog for breeding, or a show dog. Would you prefer a male or female? Puppy or adult?

If you buy from a breeder, ask him to help you with your decision. When you have settled on the dog you want, discuss with him the dog's temperament, the animal's positive and negative aspects, any health problems it might have, its feeding and grooming requirements, and whether the dog has been immunized. Reputable breeders will be willing to answer any questions you might have that pertain to the dog you have selected, and often they will make themselves available if you call for advice or if you encounter problems after you've made your purchase.

A well-balanced pup, this is Gung Ho's Ping Ki Li, owned by Alice Lawler and Peggy Kastner. This youngster is shown taking Best of Breed in a Juniors' competition, handled by Alicia Kastner.

A bit too big?
A little **too** small.
Too fuzzy for me!
Too fat to crawl.

Before you wrap it tight
And crate it home,
Behold its appetite
And room to roam.

A sloppy yap, a barking slur,
Puppy eyes to be let free,
A him? a her? an unmarked cur,
Let's pout to see its pedigree.

The perfect pet quest:
Which pup for me is best?

ANDREW DE PRISCO

Most breeders want to see their dogs placed in loving, responsible homes; they are careful about who buys their animals. So as the dog's new owner, prepare yourself for some interrogation from the breeder

Buying a puppy should not be an impulsive endeavor; it is never wise to rush out and buy just any puppy that catches your shopping eye. The more time and thought you invest, the greater your satisfaction with your new companion. And if this

Shampoos designed for a dog's sensitive skin are available at pet shops. Photo courtesy of Rolf C. Hagen Corp.

new companion is to be purely a pet, its background and early care will affect its future health and good temperament. It is always essential that you choose a properly raised puppy from healthy, well-bred stock.

You must seek out an active, sturdy puppy with bright eyes and an intelligent expression. If the puppy is friendly, that's a major plus, but you don't want one that is hyperactive nor do you want one that is dull and listless. The coat should be clean and plush, with no signs of fleas or other parasites. The premises should be clean, by sight and smell, and the proprietors should be helpful and knowledgeable. A reputable seller wants his customers satisfied and will therefore represent the puppy fairly. Let good common sense guide your purchase, and choose a reliable, well-recommended source that you know has well-satisfied customers. Don't look for a bargain, since you may end up paying many times over in future veterinarian bills, not to mention disappointment and heartache if your pet turns out not to be well.

If you feel that something is lacking in the care or condition of dogs, it is better to look elsewhere than to buy hastily and regret it afterward. Buy a healthy dog with a good disposition, one that has been

Noted for her outstanding movement is Ch. Gold's Taffy Apple Hau Jou owned by Gayle Gold of the House of Gold.

properly socialized and likes being around people.

If you cannot find the dog you want locally, write to the secretary of the national breed club or kennel club and ask for names of breeders near you or to whom you can write for information. Puppies are often shipped, sight unseen, from reputable breeders. In these instances, pictures and pedigree information are usually sent beforehand to help you decide.

Breeders can supply you with further details and helpful guidance, if you require it. Many breed clubs provide a puppy referral service, so you may want to look into this before making your final decision.

PET OR SHOW DOG

Conscientious breeders strive to maintain those desirable qualities in their breed. At the same time, they are always working to improve on what they have already achieved, and they do this by referring to the breed standard of perfection. The standard describes the ideal dog, and those animals that come close to the ideal are generally selected as show

Owners of purebred dogs too often forget that all breeds of dog are interrelated. The ancient canine that is the believed ancestor of all dogs is known as Tomarctus. As packs traveled and inhabited various lands, types evolved through the process of adaptation. Later, as dogs and man joined forces, type became further diversified. This chart sketches one commonly accepted theory of the domesticated dog's development. Where does your dog fit in? With a few exceptions, dogs evolve or change as a result of a specific functional need.

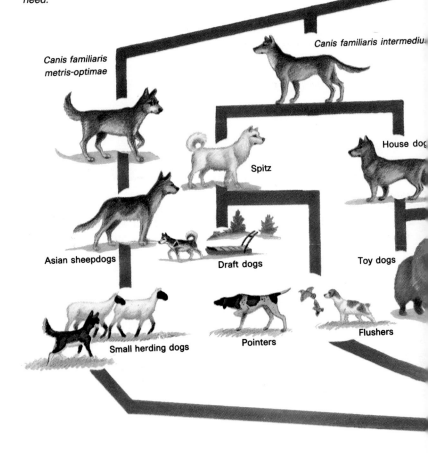

Canis familiaris intermediu.

Canis familiaris metris-optimae

Spitz

House dog

Asian sheepdogs

Draft dogs

Toy dogs

Small herding dogs

Pointers

Flushers

Tomarctus

Canis familiaris leineri

Canis familiaris inostranzewi

Russian Tracker

Molossian

Scenthounds

Sighthound
prototypes

Mastiffs

Sighthounds

Terriers

Bulldogs

Retrievers

Large herding dogs

stock; those that do not are culled and sold as pets. Keep in mind that pet-quality purebred dogs are in no way less healthy or attractive than show-quality specimens. It's just that the pet may have undesirable features (such as ears that are too large

A champion of unsurpassable acclaim, Ch. Gold's Black Magic owner-bred by Gayle and Marty Gold sired 22 champions. He was highly praised for his wonderful temperament and the consistent sparkle of his progeny.

or eyes that are the wrong color for its breed) which would be faults in the show ring. Often these so-called "flaws" are detectable only by experienced breeders or show judges. Naturally the more perfect animal, in terms of its breed standard, will cost more—even though he seems almost identical to his pet-quality littermate.

If you think you may eventually want to show your dog or raise a litter of puppies, by all means buy the best you can afford. You will save expense and disappointment later on. However, if the puppy is strictly to be a pet for the children, or a companion for you, you can afford to look for a bargain. The pup which is not show material, or the older pup for which there is often less demand, or the grown dog which is not being used for breeding are occasionally available and offer opportunities to save money. Remember that your initial investment may be a bargain, but it takes good food and care— and plenty of both—to raise a healthy, vigorous puppy through its adulthood.

Facing page: A notable trait of the Shar-pei is the purple tongue which is very visible on this specimen. This handsome dog is owned by Valerie E. Fiorella.

The price you pay for your dog is little compared to the love and devotion he will return over the many years he'll be with you. With proper care and affection, your pup should live to a ripe old age; thanks to modern veterinary science and improvements in canine nutrition, dogs today are better maintained and live longer. It is not uncommon to see dogs living well into their teens.

Generally speaking, small dogs live longer than big ones. With love and the proper care any dog will live to its optimum age. Many persons, however, opt for a particular breed because of its proven longevity. This, of course, is purely a personal decision.

MALE OR FEMALE

Let us first disregard the usual generalizations and misconceptions applied to male vs. female dogs and consider the practical concerns. If you intend to show your new dog, a male will likely closer adhere to the

Size variation in the dog family is extreme. The consideration of size must be a high priority when choosing a breed. The amount of housing, exercise, and food required, as well as the animal's lifespan are just some of the factors involved.

breed standard, though ring competition for males is stiffer. A female chosen to show cannot be spayed and the owner must contend with the bitch's heat period. If it is solely a pet—and pet animals should *not* be bred—castration or spaying is necessary. Neutered pets have longer lifespans and have a decreased risk of cancer. Males are more economical to neuter than are females. You might also consider that females are generally smaller than males, easier to housetrain, may be more family-oriented and protective of home and property. Any dog will roam—male or female—castration will not affect roaming in most cases. Males are larger and stronger, proving better guard-dog candidates. Of course, a dog of either sex, if properly trained, can make a charming, reliable, and loving pet. Male vs. female is chiefly a matter of personal preference—go with your first instinct.

ADULT OR PUP

Whether to buy a grown dog or a young puppy is another question. It is surely an undeniable pleasure to watch your dog grow from a lively pup to a mature, dignified dog. If you don't have the time to spend on the more frequent meals, housebreaking, and other training a puppy needs in order to become a dog you can be

Life Expectancy	
Dog's Age in Years	Comparative Human Age in Years
1	15
2	24
3	28
4	32
5	36
6	40
7	44
8	48
9	52
10	56
11	60
12	64
13	68
14	72
15	76
16	80
17	84
18	88
19	92
20	96
21	100

This chart is designed to provide a comparative view of ages between a dog and its human counterpart. Necessarily it is an oversimplification since larger breeds often have shorter lifespans than do average or medium-sized dogs; likewise working dogs may tend to live shorter lives than the easygoing pet dog. These factors, and many others, must be taken into account when considering this chart.

proud of, then choose an older, partly-trained adolescent or a grown dog. If you want a show dog, remember that no one, not even an expert, can predict with one hundred percent accuracy what a puppy will be like when he grows up. The dog may seem to exhibit show potential *most* of the time, but six months is the earliest age for the would-be exhibitor to select a prospect and know that its future is in the show ring.

If you have a small child, it is best to get a puppy big enough to defend itself, one not less than four or five months old.

Older children will enjoy playing with and helping to take care of a baby pup; but at less than four months, a puppy wants to do little else but eat and sleep, and he must be protected from teasing and overtiring. You cannot expect a very young child to understand that a puppy is a fragile living being; to the youngster he is a toy like his

This wonderful, huggable bundle is Fingertail Bumble, certain to tumble her way into the hearts of a number of judges. Owner, Jo Ann Webster.

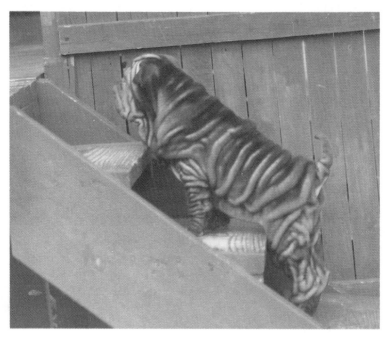

House of Treasures Oprah taking the first steps toward her championship.

stuffed dog. Children, therefore, must learn how to handle and care for their young pets.

We recommend you start with a puppy so that you can raise and train it according to the rules you have established in your own home. While a dog is young, its behavior can be more easily shaped by the owner, whereas an older dog , although trainable, may be a bit set in his ways.

WHAT TO LOOK FOR IN A PUPPY

In choosing a puppy, assuming that it comes from healthy, well-bred parents, look for one that is friendly and outgoing. The biggest pup in the litter is apt to be somewhat coarse as a grown dog, while the appealing "runt of the litter" may turn out to be a timid shadow—or have a Napoleonic complex! If you want a show dog and have no experience in choosing a prospect, study the breed standard and listen carefully to the breeder on the finer points of show conformation. A breeder's prices will be in accord with his puppies' expected worth, and he will be honest with you about each pup's potential because it is to his own advantage. He wants his top-quality show puppies placed in the public eye to reflect glory on him—and to attract future buyers. Why should he sell a potential show champion to someone who just wants a pet?

Now that you have paid your money and made your choice, you are ready to depart with puppy, papers, and instructions. Make sure that you know the youngster's feeding routine, and take along some of his food. For the trip home, place him in a comfortable, sturdy carrier. Do not drive home with a puppy on your lap! If you'll be travelling for a few hours, at the very least bring along a bottle of water from the breeder and a small water dish.

PEDIGREE AND REGISTRATION

Owners of puppies are often misled by sellers with such ruses as leading the owner to believe his dog is something special. The term *pedigree papers* is quite different from the term *registration papers*. A pedigree is nothing more than a statement made by the breeder of the dog;

If you have never been to a dog show, whether you're interested in show dogs or not, by all means—Go! An all-breed dog show will give you hands-on experience with different breeds of dog, the chance to meet their owners and breeders, and the answers to many of your questions.

Pedigree papers can trace a dog's lineage back several generations. They do not, however, guarantee that a puppy is purebred, healthy or sound.

and it is written on special pedigree blanks, which are readily available from any pet shop or breed club, with the names of several generations from which the new puppy comes. It records your puppy's ancestry and other important data, such as the pup's date of birth, its breed, its sex, its sire and dam, its breeder's name and address, and so on. If your dog has had purebred champions in his background, then the pedigree papers are valuable as evidence of the good breeding behind your dog; but if the names on the pedigree paper are meaningless, then so is the paper itself. Just because a dog has a pedigree doesn't necessarily mean he is registered with a kennel club.

Registration papers from the American Kennel Club or the United Kennel Club in the United States or The Kennel Club of Great Britain attest to the fact that the mother and father of your puppy were purebred dogs of the breed represented by your puppy and that they were registered with a particular club. Normally every registered dog also has a complete pedigree available. Registration papers, which you receive when you buy a puppy, merely enable you to register your puppy. Usually the breeder has registered only the litter, so it is the new owner's responsibility to register and name an individual pup. The papers should be filled out and sent to the appropriate address printed on the application, along with the fee required for the registration. A certificate of registration will then be sent to you.

Pedigree and registration, by the way, have nothing to do with licensing, which is a local regulation applying to purebred and mongrel alike. Find out what the local ordinance is in your town or city and how it applies to your dog; then buy a license and keep it on your dog's collar for identification.

This handsome Shar-pei is Ch. Blackwitch's Charlie Jenning. He finished his championship at less than one year of age. Owner, May Jennings.

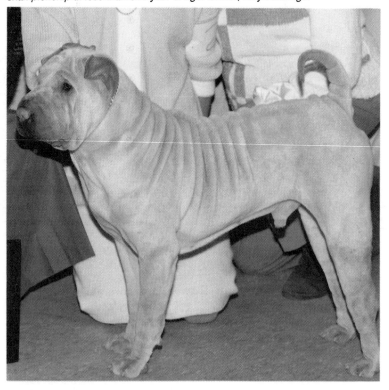

The New Family Member

Taking Winners here at Windy City All-Breed Match, this is Ch. Stroh's Brewed at Blackwitch. Owner, Denise A. Beagle, Blackwitch Farms.

At long last, the day you have all been waiting for, your new puppy will make its grand entrance into your home. Before you bring your companion to its new residence, however, you must plan carefully for its arrival. Keep in mind that the puppy will need time to adjust to life with a different owner. He may seem a bit apprehensive about the strange surroundings in which he finds himself, having spent the first few weeks of life with his dam and littermates, but in a couple of days, with love and patience on your part, the transition will be complete.

First impressions are important, especially from the puppy's point of view, and these may very well set the pattern of his future relationship with you. You must be consistent in the

The puppy's bed will provide a place of refuge and privacy. Make sure that the puppy's toilet needs have been met before sending him to bed for the night.

way you handle your pet so that he learns what is expected of him. He must come to trust and respect you as his keeper and master. Provide him with proper care and attention, and you will be rewarded with a loyal companion for many years. Considering the needs of your puppy and planning ahead will surely make the change from his former home to his new one easier.

ADVANCE PREPARATION

In preparing for your puppy's arrival, perhaps more important than anything else is to find out from the seller how the pup was maintained. What brand of food was offered and when and how often was the puppy fed? Has

BASIC PUPPY NEEDS

- Canned and dry food/diet schedule
- Feeding and water bowls
- Carrying/sleeping crate
- Bed
- Collar and leash
- Grooming supplies (brushes, shampoo, etc.)
- Outdoor lead and/or pen
- Muzzle/first-aid kit
- Flea collar and preparations
- Safe chew products (Nylabone®, Gumabone®)
- Edible chew products (treats/rewards)

the pup been housebroken; if so, what method was employed? Attempt to continue whatever routine was started by the person from whom you bought your puppy; then, gradually, you can make those changes that suit you and your lifestyle. If, for example, the puppy has been paper trained, plan to stock up on newspaper. Place this newspaper toilet facility in a selected spot so that your puppy learns to use the designated area as his "bathroom." And keep on hand a supply of the dog food to which he is accustomed, as a sudden switch to new food could cause digestive upsets.

Another consideration is sleeping and resting quarters. Be sure to supply a dog bed for your pup, and introduce him to his special cozy corner so that he

This chart lists some of the many items that the dog owner should have on hand before he brings home his new charge.

knows where to retire when he feels like taking a snooze. You'll need to buy a collar (or harness) and leash, a safe chew item (such as Nylabone® or Gumabone®), and a few grooming tools as well. A couple of sturdy feeding dishes, one for food and one for water, will be needed; and it will be necessary, beforehand, to set up a feeding station.

FINDING A VETERINARIAN

An important part of your preparations should include finding a local veterinarian who can provide quality health care in the form of routine check-ups, inoculations, and prompt medical attention in case of illness or an emergency. Find out if the animal you have selected has been vaccinated against canine diseases, and make certain you secure all health certificates at the time of purchase. This information will be valuable to your veterinarian, who will want to know the puppy's complete medical history. Incidentally, don't wait until your puppy becomes sick before you seek the services of a vet; make an appointment for your pup before or soon after he takes up residence with you so that he starts out with a clean bill of health in his new home.

CHILDREN AND PUPPIES

Prepare the young members of the household on pet care. Children should learn not only to love their charges but to respect them and treat them with the consideration one would give all living things. It must be emphasized to youngsters that the puppy has certain needs, just as humans have, and all family members must take an active role in ensuring that these needs are met. Someone must feed the puppy. Someone must walk him a couple of times a day or clean up after him if he is trained to relieve himself on newspaper. Someone must groom his coat, clean his ears, and clip his nails from time to time. Someone

must see to it that the puppy gets sufficient exercise and attention each day.

A child who has a pet to care for learns responsibility; nonetheless, parental guidance is an essential part of his learning experience. Many a child has been known to "love a pet to death," squeezing and hugging the animal in ways which are irritating or even painful. Others have been found guilty of teasing, perhaps unintentionally, and disturbing their pet while the animal is eating or resting. One must teach a child, therefore, when and how to gently stroke and fondle a puppy. In time, the child can learn how to carefully pick up and handle the pup. A dog should always be supported with both hands, *not* lifted by the scruff of the neck. One hand placed under the chest, between the front legs, and the other hand supporting the dog's rear end will be comfortable and will restrain the animal as you hold and carry him. Always demonstrate to children the proper way to lift a dog.

BE A GOOD NEIGHBOR

For the sake of your dog's safety and well being, don't allow him to wander onto the property of others. Keep him confined at all times to your own yard or indoors where he won't become a nuisance. Consider what

Evident in this photo, the adult Shar-pei is much less wrinkled than the Shar-pei puppy although no less irresistible.

Clockwise from upper right: *pokeweed, jimson weed, foxglove, and yew.* If ingested, any toxic plant can be dangerous to your dog.

ROVER WILL NOT BE HARMED IF YOU FOLLOW MY INSTRUCTIONS

AMF

Dog theft is not an uncommon event. Dognappers will steal either a purebred or mongrel puppy so all owners must always be wary.

dangers lie ahead for an unleashed dog that has total freedom of the great outdoors, particularly when he is unsupervised by his master. There are cars and trucks to dodge on the streets and highways. There are stray animals with which to wrangle. There are poisons all around, such as car antifreeze in driveways or toxic plants and shrubs, which, if swallowed, could prove fatal. There are dognappers and sadistic people who may steal or bring harm to your beloved pet. In short, there are all sorts of nasty things waiting to hurt him. Did you know that if your dog consumes rotting garbage, there is the possibility he could go into shock or even die? And are you aware that a dog left to roam in a wooded area or field could become infected with any number of parasites if he plays with or ingests some small prey, such as a rabbit, that might be carrying these parasitic organisms? A thorn from a rosebush imbedded in the dog's foot pad, tar from a newly paved road stuck to his coat, and a wound inflicted by a wild animal all can be avoided if you take the precaution of keeping your dog in a safe enclosure where he will be protected from such dangers. Don't let your dog run loose; he is likely to stray from home and get into all sorts of trouble.

The New Family Member

GETTING ACQUAINTED

Plan to bring your new pet home in the morning so that by nightfall he will have had some time to become acquainted with you and his new environment. Avoid introducing the pup to the family around holiday time, since all of the extra excitement will only add to the confusion and frighten him. Let the puppy enter your home on a day when the

Resist the temptation to handle him too much during these first few days. And, if there are other dogs or animals around the house, make certain all are properly introduced. If you observe fighting among the animals, or some other problem, you may have to separate all parties until they learn to accept one another. Remember that neglecting your other pets while

routine is normal. For those people who work during the week, a Saturday morning is an ideal time to bring the puppy to his new home; this way he has the entire weekend to make adjustments before being left alone for a few hours, come Monday morning.

Let the puppy explore, under your watchful eye of course, and let him come to know his new home without stress and fear.

Pictured here as a puppy, Ch. Temple Toi Talala—a Shar-pei of particular promise owned by Ann Coleman, Tail's End Shar-Pei.

Facing page: *The appeal and charm of the Chinese Shar-pei puppy are seemingly unending. Defying description and sensibility, these two puppies exemplify such ineffability.*

showering the new puppy with extra attention will only cause animosity and jealousy. Make an effort to pay special attention to the other animals as well.

On that eventful first night, try not to give in and let the puppy sleep with you; otherwise, this could become a difficult habit to break. Let him cry and whimper, even if it means a night of restlessness for the entire family. Some people have had success with putting a doll or a hot water bottle wrapped in a towel in the puppy's bed as a surrogate mother, while others have placed a ticking alarm clock in the bed to simulate the heartbeat of the pup's dam and littermates. Remember that this furry little fellow is used to the warmth and security of his mother and siblings, so the adjustment to sleeping alone will take time. Select a location away from drafts and away from the feeding station for placement of his dog bed. Keep in mind, also, that the bed should be roomy enough for him to stretch out in; as he grows older, you may need to supply a larger one.

Prior to the pup's arrival, set up his room and partition it the way you would to keep an infant out of a particular area. You may want to keep his bed, his feeding station, and his toilet area all in the same room—in separate locations—or you may want to set the feeding station up in your kitchen, where meals for all family members are served. Whatever you decide, do it ahead of time so you will have that much less to worry about when your puppy finally moves in with you.

Above all else, be patient with your puppy as he adjusts to life in his new home. If you purchase a pup that is not housebroken, you will have to spend time with the dog—just as you would with a small child—until he develops proper toilet habits. Even a housebroken puppy may feel nervous in strange new surroundings and have an occasional accident. Praise and encouragement will elicit far better results than punishment or scolding. Remember that your puppy wants nothing more than to please you, thus he is anxious to learn the behavior that is required of him.

Feeding Requirements

Perhaps more than any other single aspect of your dog's development, proper feeding requires an educated and responsible dog owner. The importance of nutrition on your dog's bone and muscle growth cannot be overemphasized.

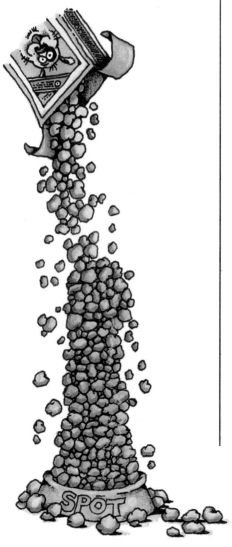

Soon after your puppy comes to live with you, he will need to be fed. Remember to ask the seller what foods were given to the youngster and stay with that diet for a while. It is important for the puppy to keep eating and to avoid skipping a meal, so entice him with the food to which he is accustomed. If you prefer to switch to some other brand of dog food, each day begin to add small quantities of the new brand to the usual food offering. Make the portions of the new food progressively larger until the pup is weaned from his former diet.

What should you feed the puppy and how often? His diet is really quite simple and relatively inexpensive to prepare. Puppies need to be fed small portions at frequent intervals, since they are growing and their activity level is high. You must ensure that your pup gains weight steadily; with an adult dog, however, growth slows down and weight must be regulated to prevent obesity and a host of other problems. At one time, it was thought that home-cooked meals were the answer, with daily rations of meat,

Choosing a quality dog food from your pet shop is easy—deciding how much to feed may not be as straightforward. Feedings must always be carefully monitored.

vegetables, egg yolk, cereal, cheese, brewer's yeast, and vitamin supplements. With all of the nutritionally complete commercial dog food products readily available, these time-consuming preparations really are unnecessary now. A great deal of money and research has resulted in foods that we can serve our dogs with confidence and pride; and most of these commercial foods have been developed along strict guidelines according to the size, weight, and age of your dog. These products are reasonably priced,

The first days of puppy training can be simplified by having the right accommodations. Specially designed puppy feeders like the ones shown here will make your puppy's meals clean and enjoyable. Photo courtesy of Rolf C. Hagen Corp.

easy to find, and convenient to store.

THE PUPPY'S MEALS

After a puppy has been fully weaned from its mother until approximately three months of age, it needs to be fed four times a day. In the morning and evening offer kibble (dog meal) soaked in hot water or broth, to which you have added some canned meat-based food or fresh raw meat cut into small chunks. At noon and bedtime feed him a bit of kibble or wholegrain cereal moistened with milk (moistening, by the way, makes the food easier to digest, since dogs don't typically chew their food). From the age of three to six months, increase the portion size and offer just three meals—one milk

An extraordinary specimen, this is three-month-old Remington's Earth Angel, possibly one of the most outstanding puppies to be produced at this kennel.

offer just three meals—one milk and two meat. At six months, two meals are sufficient; at one year, a single meal can be given, supplemented with a few dry biscuits in the morning and evening. During the colder months, especially if your dog is active, you might want to mix in some wheat germ oil or corn oil or bacon drippings with the meal to add extra calories. Remember to keep a bowl of cool, fresh water on hand always to help your dog regulate its body temperature and to aid in digestion.

From one year on, you may continue feeding the mature dog a single meal (in the evening, perhaps, when you have your supper), or you may prefer to divide this meal in two, offering half in the morning and the other half at night. Keep in mind that while puppies require foods in small chunks, or nuggets, older dogs can handle larger pieces of food at mealtime. Discuss your dog's feeding schedule with your veterinarian; he can make suggestions about the right diet for your particular canine friend.

COMPARISON SHOPPING

With so many fine dog-food products on the market today, there is something for everyone's pet. You may want to serve dry food "as is" or mix it with warm water or broth. Perhaps you'll choose to combine dry food with fresh or canned preparations. Some canned foods contain all meat, but they are not complete; others are mixtures of meat and grains, which have been fortified with additional nutrients to make them more complete and balanced. There are also various packaged foods that can be served alone or as supplements and that can be left out for a few hours without spoiling. This self-feeding method, which works well for dogs that are not prone to weight problems, allows the animal to serve himself whenever he feels hungry. Many people who work during the day find these dry or semi-moist rations convenient to use, and these foods are great to bring along if you travel with your dog.

Be sure to read the labels carefully before you make your dog-food purchases. Most

Feeder bins are used by many kennel owners as well as pet owners. These devices help to conveniently store and distribute dry foods in a sanitary, efficient way.

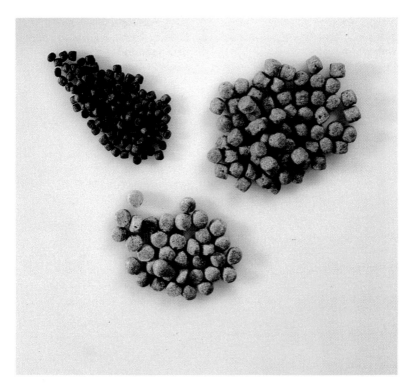

Pet shops offer a variety of dry kibbles. Though the nutritional values of these foods are essentially equivalent, compare the manufacturer's labels.

reputable pet-food manufacturers list the ingredients and the nutritional content right on the can or package. Instructions are usually included so that you will know how much to feed your dog to keep him thriving and in top condition. A varied, well-balanced diet that supplies the proper amounts of protein, carbohydrate, fat, vitamins, minerals, and water is important to keep your puppy healthy and to guarantee his normal development. Adjustments to the diet can be made, under your veterinarian's supervision, according to the individual puppy, his rate of growth, his activity level, and so on. Liquid or powder vitamin and mineral supplements, or those in tablet form, are available and can be given if you need to feel certain that the diet is balanced.

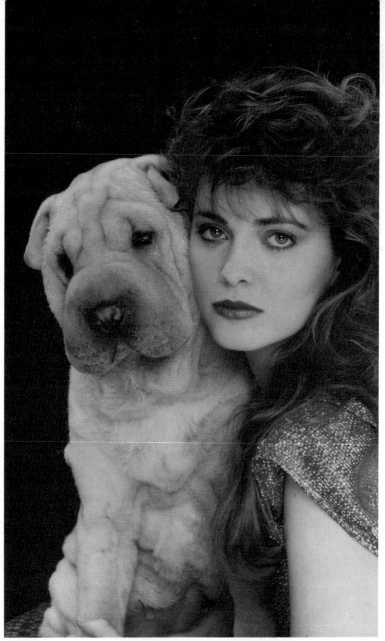

The Shar-Pei's unique appearance and delightful disposition have made the breed quite in vogue in recent times. Here Legibach's Lady Prunella at six months of age enjoys some very special attention. Owners, Pat and Gina Leone.

DEVELOPING GOOD EATING HABITS

Try to serve your puppy his meals at the same time each day and in the same location so that he will get used to his daily routine and develop good eating habits. A bit of raw egg, cottage cheese, or table scraps (leftover food from your own meals) can be offered from time to time; but never accustom your dog to eating human "junk food." Cake, candy, chocolate, soda, and other snack foods are for people, not dogs. Besides, these foods provide only "empty" calories that your pet doesn't need if he is to stay healthy. Avoid offering spicy, fried, fatty, or starchy foods; rather, offer leftover meats, vegetables, and gravies. Get in the habit of feeding your puppy or your grown dog his *own* daily meals of dog food. If ever you are in doubt about what foods and how much to serve, consult your veterinarian.

Four Paws Good 'N Plenty Feeder is designed to hold approximately 2 pounds of food. The Good 'N Plenty Waterer holds a generous 3 quarts. Both are designed for easy dismantling and cleaning.

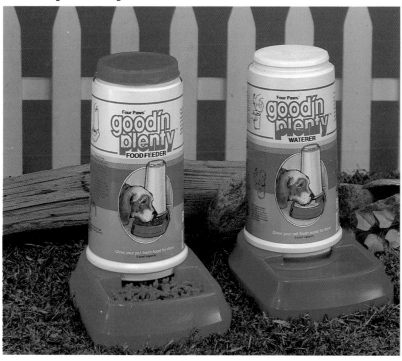

FEEDING GUIDELINES

Some things to bear in mind with regard to your dog's feeding regimen follow.

• Nutritional balance, provided by many commercial dog foods, is vital; avoid feeding a one-sided all-meat diet. Variety in the kinds of meat (beef, lamb, chicken, liver) or cereal grains (wheat, oats, corn) that you offer your dog is of secondary importance compared to the balance or "completeness" of dietary components.

• Always refrigerate opened canned food so that it doesn't spoil. Remember to remove all uneaten portions of canned or moistened food from the feeding dish as soon as the pup has finished his meal. Discard the leftover food immediately and thoroughly wash and dry the feeding dish, as a dirty dish is a breeding ground for harmful germs.

• When offering dry foods, always keep a supply of water on hand for your dog. Water should be made available at all times, even if dry foods are not left out for self-feeding. Each

Feeding your dog is made easy by the use of sturdy non-tip, easy-clean bowls. Pet shops offer the best selection of colors, styles and sizes.

day the water dish should be washed with soap and hot water, rinsed well, and dried; a refill of clean, fresh water should be provided daily.

• Food and water should be served at room temperature, neither too hot nor too cold, so that it is more palatable for your puppy.

• Serve your pup's meals in sturdy hard-plastic, stainless steel, or earthenware containers, ones that won't tip over as the dog gulps his food down. Some bowls and dishes are weighted to prevent spillage, while others fit neatly into holders which offer support. Feeding dishes should be large enough to hold each meal.

• Whenever the nutritional needs of your dog change—that is to say, when it grows older or if it becomes ill, obese, or pregnant; or if it starts to nurse its young—special diets are in order. Always contact your vet for advice on these special dietary requirements.

• Feed your puppy at the same regular intervals each day; reserve treats for special occasions or, perhaps, to reward good behavior during training

sessions.

• Hard foods, such as biscuits and dog meal, should be offered regularly. Chewing on these hard, dry morsels helps the dog keep its teeth clean and its gums conditioned.

• Never overfeed your dog. If given the chance, he will accept

New treats on the block by Nylabone®. These Chooz® crunchy dog bones are delectable and affordable.

and relish every in-between-meal tidbit you offer him. This pampering will only put extra weight on your pet and cause him to be unhealthy in the long run.

• Do not encourage your dog to beg for food from the table while you are eating your meals.

• Food can be effectively used by the owner to train the dog. Doggie treats are practical and often nutritional—choose your chew treats choosily.

FEEDING CHART

Age and No. of Feedings Per Day	Weight in Lbs.	Weight in Kg.	Caloric Requirement kcal M.E./Day
Puppies—Weaning to 3 months Four per day	1–3 3–6 6–12 12–20 15–30	.5–1.4 1.4–2.7 2.7–5.4 5.4–9.1 6.8–13.6	124–334 334–574 574–943 943–1384 1113–1872
Puppies—3 to 6 months Three per day	3–10 5–15 12–25 20–40 30–70	1.4–4.5 2.3–6.8 5.4–11.3 9.1–18.2 13.6–31.8	334–816 494–1113 943–1645 1384–2352 1872–3542
Puppies—6 to 12 months Two per day	6–12 12–25 20–50 40–70 70–100	2.7–5.4 5.4–11.3 9.1–22.7 18.2–31.8 31.8–45.4	574–943 943–1645 1384–2750 2352–3542 3542–4640
Normally Active Adults One or two per day	6–12 12–25 25–50 50–90 90–175	2.7–5.4 5.4–11.3 11.3–22.7 22.7–40.8 40.8–79.4	286–472 472–823 823–1375 1375–2151 2151–3675

This chart presents general parameters of the dog's caloric requirements, based on weight. The total caloric intake comes from a complete, balanced diet of quality foods. To assist owners, dog food companies generally provide the nutritional information to their product right on the label.

Accommodations

Puppies newly weaned from their mother and siblings should be kept warm at all times. As they get older, they can be acclimated gradually to cooler temperatures. When you purchase your dog, find out from the seller whether he is hardy and can withstand the rigors of outdoor living. Many breeds have been known to adapt well to a surprising number of environments, so long as they are given time to adjust. If your pup is to be an indoor companion, perhaps a dog bed in the corner of the family room will suffice; or you may want to invest in a crate for him to call his "home" whenever he needs to be confined for short intervals. You might plan to partition off a special room, or part of a room, for your pooch; or you may find that a heated garage or finished basement works well as your dog's living quarters. If your breed can tolerate living outside, you may want to buy or build him his own dog house with an attached run. It might be feasible to place his house in your fenced-in backyard. The breed that can live outdoors fares well when given access to some sort of warm, dry shelter during periods of inclement weather. As you begin thinking about where your canine friend will spend most of his time, you'll want to consider his breed, his age, his temperament, his need for exercise, and the money, space, and resources you have available to house him.

A bed for your dog gives him a place to call his own. His bed should be placed in a warm, dry, draft-free area.

THE DOG BED

In preparing for your puppy's arrival, it is recommended that a dog bed be waiting for him so that he has a place to sleep and rest. If you have provided him with his own bed or basket, ensure that it is placed in a warm, dry, draft-free spot that is private but at the same time near the center of family activity. Refrain from placing his bed near the feed and water dishes or his toilet area. You may want to give your puppy something with which to snuggle, such as a laundered towel or blanket or an article of old clothing. Some dogs have been known to chew apart their beds and bedding, but you can easily channel this chewing energy into more constructive behavior simply by supplying him with some safe toys or a Nylabone® pacifier for gnawing. Pet shops stock dog beds, among other supplies that you might need for your pup. Select a bed that is roomy, comfortable, and easy to clean, keeping in mind that you may have to replace the smaller bed with a larger one as the puppy grows to adulthood. Remember to clean and disinfect the bed and sleeping area from time to time, as these can become parasitic playgrounds for fleas, lice, mites, and the like.

Beds can have personality. Pet shops offer many different bedding options to the owner willing to explore.

The wire crate is a most effective means to accelerate housebreaking and is the safest way to ensure that the puppy is safe when he cannot be supervised.

THE CRATE

Although many dog lovers may cringe at the mere mention of the word *crate,* thinking of it as a cage or a cruel means of confinement, this handy piece of equipment can be put to good use for puppies and grown dogs alike. Even though you may love your dog to an extraordinary degree, you may not want him to have free reign of the house, particularly when you are not home to supervise him. If used properly, a crate can restrict your dog when it is not convenient to have him underfoot, *i.e.,* when guests are visiting or during your mealtimes.

A surprising number of dog owners, who originally had negative feelings about crating their dogs, have had great success using crates. The crate itself serves as a bed, provided it is furnished with bedding material, or it can be used as an indoor dog house. Not all dogs readily accept crates or being confined in them for short

Four Paws offers a wide range of shampoos for every need: from flea and tick to medicated and many others. All shampoos are pH balanced for a gentle yet effective cleaning.

intervals, so for these dogs, another means of restriction must be found. But for those dogs that do adjust to spending time in these structures, the crate can be useful in many ways. The animal can be confined for a few hours while you are away from home or at work, or you can bring your crated dog along with you in the car when you travel or go on vacation. Crates also prove handy as carriers whenever you have to transport a sick dog to the veterinarian.

Most crates are made of sturdy wire or plastic, and some of the collapsible models can be conveniently stored or folded so that they can be moved easily from room to room or from inside the house to the yard on a warm, sunny day. If you allow your puppy or grown dog to become acquainted with its crate by cleverly propping the door open and leaving some of his favorite toys inside, in no time he will come to regard the crate as his own doggie haven. As with a dog bed, place the crate away from drafts in a dry, warm spot; refrain from placing food and water dishes in it, as these only crowd the space and offer opportunity for spillage.

If you need to confine your puppy so that he can't get into mischief while you're not home, remember to consider the animal's needs at all times. Select a large crate, one in which the dog can stand up and move around comfortably; in fact, bigger is better in this context. Never leave the animal confined for more than a few hours at a time without letting him out to exercise, play, and, if necessary, relieve himself. Never crate a dog for ten hours, for example, unless you keep the door to the crate open so that he can get out for food and water and to stretch a bit. If long intervals of confinement are necessary, consider placing the unlatched crate in a partitioned section of your house or apartment.

Crates have become the answer for many a dog owner faced with the dilemma of either getting rid of a destructive dog or living with him despite his bad habits. People who have neither the time nor the patience to train their dogs, or to modify undesirable behavior patterns, can at least restrain their pets during the times they can't be there to supervise. So long as the crate is used in a humane fashion, whereby a dog is

Traveling crates can provide safe and easy transport for your dog. Ventilation for travel is a most important consideration.

confined for no more than a few hours at any one time, it can figure importantly in a dog owner's life. Show dogs, incidentally, learn at an early age that much time will be spent in and out of crates while they are on the show circuit. Many canine celebrities are kept in their crates until they are called to ringside, and they spend many hours crated to and from the shows.

THE DOG HOUSE

These structures, often made of wood, should be sturdy and offer enough room for your dog to stretch out in when it rests or sleeps. Dog houses that are elevated or situated on a platform protect the animal from cold and dampness that may seep through the ground. For the breeds that are temperature hardy and will live outdoors, a dog house is an excellent option for daytime occupancy. Owners who cannot provide indoor accommodations for their chosen dog should consider a smaller breed since no dog should lead an exclusively outdoor existence.

If you have no option but to accommodate your dog with only an outdoor house, it will be necessary to provide him with a more elaborate house, one that really protects him from the elements. Make sure the dog's house is constructed of waterproof materials. Furnish

The pet trade offers many commercially made dog houses and other outdoor living structures that make great temporary accommodations for your pet.

Indoor-outdoor dog houses offer pest-free, sanitary conditions for your dog. These attractive living options can be acquired from pet shops or supply outlets.

him with sufficient bedding to burrow into on a chilly night and provide extra insulation to keep out drafts and wet weather. Add a partition (a kind of room divider which separates the entry area from the main sleeping space) inside his house or attach a swinging door to the entrance to help keep him warm when he is inside his residence. The swinging door facilitates entry to and from the dog house, while at the same time it provides protection, particularly from wind and drafts.

Some fortunate owners whose yards are enclosed by high fencing allow their dogs complete freedom within the boundaries of their property. In these situations, a dog can leave his dog house and get all the exercise he wants. Of course such a large space requires more effort to keep it clean. An alternative to complete backyard freedom is a dog kennel or run which attaches to or surrounds the dog's house. This restricts some forms of movement, such as running, perhaps, but it does provide ample room for walking, climbing, jumping, and stretching. Another option is to fence off part of the yard and place the dog house in the enclosure. If you need to tether your dog to its house, make certain to use a fairly long lead so as not to hamper the animal's need to move and exercise his limbs.

An anchored lead can provide efficient temporary restraint. This is not a viable substitute for a fenced-in yard and no dog should be left unsupervised on such a lead for any length of time.

CLEANLINESS

No matter where your dog lives, either in or out of your home, be sure to keep him in surroundings that are as clean and sanitary as possible. His excrement should be removed and disposed of every day without fail. No dog should be forced to lie in his own feces. If your dog lives in his own house, the floor should be swept occasionally and the bedding should be changed regularly if it becomes soiled. Food and water dishes need to be scrubbed with hot water and detergent and rinsed well to remove all traces of soap. The water dish should be refilled with a supply of fresh water. The dog and his environment must be kept free of parasites (especially fleas and mosquitoes, which can carry disease) with products designed to keep these pests under control. Dog crates need frequent scrubbing, too, as do the floors of kennels and runs. Your pet must be kept clean and comfortable at all times; if you exercise strict sanitary control, you will keep disease and parasite infestation to a minimum.

EXERCISE

A well-balanced diet and regular medical attention from a qualified veterinarian are essential in promoting good health for your dog, but so is daily exercise to keep him fit and mentally alert. Dogs that have been confined all day while their owners are at work or school need special attention. There should be some time set aside each day for play—a romp with a family member, perhaps. Not everyone is lucky enough to let his dog run through an open meadow or along a sandy beach, but even a ten-minute walk in the fresh air will do. Dogs that are house-bound, particularly those that live in apartments, need to be walked out-of-doors after each meal so that they can relieve themselves. Owners can make this daily ritual more pleasant both for themselves and their canine companions by combining the walk with a little "roughhousing," that is to say, a bit of fun and togetherness.

Whenever possible, take a stroll to an empty lot, a playground, or a nearby park. Attach a long lead to your dog's collar, and let him run and jump and tone his body through aerobic activity. This will help him burn calories and will keep him trim, and it will also help relieve tension and stress that may have had a chance to develop while you were away all day. For people who work Monday through Friday,

weekend jaunts can be especially beneficial, since there will be more time to spend with your canine friend. You might want to engage him in a simple game of fetch with a stick or a rubber ball. Even such basic tricks as rolling over, standing on the hindlegs, or jumping up (all of which can be done inside

Four Paws Stain & Odor Remover contains active enzymes to remove tough urine stains and the odor that attracts puppies to the previously soiled area.

the home as well) can provide additional exercise. But if you plan to challenge your dog with a real workout to raise his heart rate, remember not to push him too hard without first warming up with a brisk walk. Don't forget to "cool him down" afterwards with a rhythmic trot until his heart rate returns to normal. Some dog owners jog with their dogs or take them along on bicycle excursions.

At the very least, however, play with your dog every day to keep him in good shape physically and mentally. If you can walk him outdoors, or better

yet run with him in a more vigorous activity, by all means do it. Don't neglect your pet and leave him confined for long periods without attention from you or time for exercise.

EXERCISING FOR YOU AND YOUR DOG

Dogs are like people. They come in three weights: overweight, underweight, and the correct weight. It is fair to say that most dogs are in better shape than most humans who own them. The reason for this is that most dogs accept exercise without objection—

The most popular in flying discs designed especially for dogs is the Nylabone Frisbee®, a toy that outlasts plastic discs by ten times. The molded dog bone on the top makes for easy retrieves by your dog.

people do not! Follow your dog's lead towards exercise and the complete enjoyment of the outdoors—your dog is the ideal work-out partner. There are toys at your local pet shop which are designed just for that purpose: to allow you to play and exercise with your dog. Here are a few recommended exercise toys for you and your dog.

Frisbee® Flying Discs® Most dog owners capitalize on the dog's natural instinct to fetch or retrieve, and the Frisbee® flying disc is standard fare for play. The original Frisbee® is composed of polyethylene plastic, ideal for flying and great for games of catch between two humans. Since humans don't usually chew on their flying discs, there is no need for a "chew-worthy" construction material. Dogs, on the other hand, do chew on their Frisbees® and therefore should not be allowed to play with a standard original Frisbee®. These discs will be destroyed quickly by the dog and the rigid plastic can cause intestinal complications.

Nylon Discs More suitable for playing with dogs are the Frisbee® discs that are constructed from nylon. These durable Frisbee® discs are designed especially for dogs and the nearly indestructible

manufacturing makes them ideal for aggressive chewing dogs. For play with dogs, the nylon discs called Nylabone Frisbee® are guaranteed to last ten times as long as the regular plastic Frisbee®. Owners should

Made of durable and flexible polyurethane, the Gumabone® Frisbees® prove chew-worthy and good-smelling to dogs. These and other Nylabone® discs are available in pet shops and other stores.

carefully consider the size of the nylon Frisbee® they purchase. A rule of thumb is choose the largest disc that your dog can comfortably carry. Nylabone manufactures two

Dogs enjoy toys they can carry around. The Gumaring® is a favorite plaything for many dogs.

The Tug Toy from Gumabone® is a flavorable exercise device that can be enjoyed by dog and owner.

sizes only—toy and large—so the choice should be apparent.

Polyurethane Flexible Floppy Flying Discs The greatest advance in flying discs came with the manufacture of these discs from polyurethane. The polyurethane is so soft that it doesn't hurt you, your dog, or the window it might strike accidentally. The polyurethane Gumadisc® is floppy and soft. It can be folded and fits into your pocket. It is also much tougher than cheap plastics, and most pet shops guarantee that it will last ten times longer than cheap plastic discs.

Making the polyurethane discs even more suited to dog play is the fact that many of the Gumabone® Frisbee® Flexible Fly Discs have the advantage of a dog bone molded on the top. Very often a Frisbee® without the bone molded on the top is difficult for a dog to pick up when it lands on a flat surface. The molded ones enable the dog to grasp it with his mouth or turn it with his paw. Dogs love pawing at the bone and even chew on it occasionally.

This product has one further capacity—it doubles

as a temporary drinking dish while out running, hiking and playing. The Gumabone Frisbee® flyers may also be flavored or scented, besides being annealed, so your dog can find it more easily if it should get lost in woods or tall grass.

Flying discs manufactured by the Nylabone® Company may cost more than some of its imitators, but an owner can be assured that the product will last and not be quickly destroyed.

(100 feet) is more than enough room. You throw the disc to each other, arousing your dog's interest as he tries to catch it.

Dental floss devices from Nylabone® serve two excellent purposes: good exercise and clean teeth.

With most flying discs made for dogs comes an instruction booklet on how to use the disc with your canine friend. Basically, you play with the dog and the disc so the dog knows the disc belongs to him. Then you throw it continuously, increasing the distance, so that the dog fetches it and brings it back to you.

The exercise for you comes in when your dog stops fetching it, or when you have a partner. The two of you play catch. You stand as far apart as available space allows—usually 30–35 m

When the disc is dropped or veers off, the dog grabs it and brings it back (hopefully). Obviously you will have to run to catch the disc before your dog does.

There are contests held all over the world where distance, height, and other characteristics are measured competitively. Ask your local pet shop to help you locate a Frisbee® Club near you.

*Frisbee® is a trademark of the Kransco Company, California, and is used for their brand of flying disc.

Tug Toys A tug toy is a hard rubber, cheap plastic, or polyurethane toy which allows a dog and his owner to have a game of tug-o-war. The owner grips one end while the dog grips the other—then they pull. The polyurethane flexible tug toy is the best on the market at the present time. Your pet shop will have one to show you. The polyurethane toys are clear in color and stay soft forever. Cheap plastic tug toys are indisputably dangerous, and the hard-rubber tug toys get brittle too fast and are too stiff for most dogs; however, there *is* a difference in price—just ask the advice of any pet shop operator.

It pays to invest in entertainment toys and exercise devices which are marketed particularly for dogs. These products outlast everyday play things and are much safer for your pet. The Gumaball® is a great example of a dog toy worth the price of admission.

Balls Nobody has to tell you about playing ball with your dog. The reminder you may need is that you should not throw the ball where traffic might interfere with the dog's catching or fetching of it. The ball should not be cheap plastic (a dog's worst enemy as far as toys are concerned) but made of a substantial material. Balls made of nylon are practically indestructible, but they are very hard and must be rolled, never thrown. The same balls made of polyurethane are great—they bounce and are soft. The Nylaballs® and Gumaballs® are scented and flavored, and dogs can easily find them when lost.

Other manufacturers make balls of almost every substance, including plastic, cotton, and wood. Soft balls, baseballs, tennis balls, and so on, have all been used by dog owners who want their dogs to play with them in a game of catch. A strong caveat is that you use only those balls made especially for dogs.

Preventive Dental Care

ALL DOGS NEED TO CHEW

Puppies and young dogs need something with resistance to chew on while their teeth and jaws are developing—to cut the puppy teeth, to induce growth of the permanent teeth under the puppy teeth, to assist in getting rid of the puppy teeth on time, to help the permanent teeth through the gums, to assure

An artist's representation of the calculus index, ranging from index rating 4 (topmost drawing) through index rating 1 (lowest drawing).

4 *Buccal crown covered*
3 *⅔ crown covered*
2 *⅓ crown covered*
1 *Only gingival margin covered*
0 *No calculus evident*

normal jaw development and to settle the permanent teeth solidly in the jaws.

The adult dog's desire to chew stems from the instinct for tooth cleaning, gum massage, and jaw exercise—plus the need to vent periodic doggie tensions. . . . A pacifier if you will!

Dental caries, as they affect the teeth of humans, are virtually unknown in dogs; but tartar (calculus) accumulates on the teeth of dogs, particularly at the gum line, more rapidly than on the teeth of humans. These accumulations, if not removed, bring irritation and then infection, which erode the tooth enamel and ultimately destroy the teeth at the roots. It is important that you take your dog to your local veterinarian for periodic dental examinations.

Tooth and jaw development will normally continue until the dog is more than a year old—but sometimes much longer, depending upon the dog, its chewing exercise, rate of calcium utilization and many other factors, known and unknown, which affect the development of individual dogs. Diseases, like distemper for example, may sometimes arrest development of the teeth and jaws, which may resume months or even years later.

This is why dogs, especially puppies and young dogs, will

often destroy valuable property when their chewing instinct is not diverted from their owners' possessions, particularly during the widely varying critical period for young dogs. Saving your possessions from destruction, assuring proper development of teeth and jaws, providing for "interim" tooth cleaning and gum massage, and channeling doggie tensions into a non-destructive outlet are, therefore, all dependent upon the dog's having something suitable for chewing readily available when his instinct tells him to chew. If your purposes, and those of your dog, are to be accomplished, what you provide for chewing must be desirable from the doggie viewpoint, have the necessary functional qualities, and, above all, be safe.

It is very important that dogs be prohibited from chewing on anything they can break or indigestible things from which they can bite sizeable chunks. Sharp pieces, such as those from a bone which can be broken by a dog, may pierce the intestinal wall and kill. Indigestible things which can be bitten off in chunks, such as toys made of rubber compound or cheap plastic, may cause an intestinal stoppage; if not regurgitated, they are certain to bring painful death unless surgery is promptly performed.

NATURAL CHEW BONES

Strong natural bones, such as 4- to 8-inch lengths of round shin bone from mature beef—either the kind you can get from your butcher or one of the varieties available commercially in pet stores—may serve your dog's teething needs, if his mouth is large enough to handle them effectively, *but,* constant chewing on hard bones wears down a dog's teeth. Natural bones are very abrasive and should be used sparingly.

You may be tempted to give your puppy a smaller bone and he may not be able to break it when you do, but puppies grow rapidly and the power of their jaws constantly increases until maturity. This means that a growing dog may break one of the smaller bones at any time, swallow the pieces and die painfully before you realize what is wrong.

Many people have the mistaken notion that their dog's teeth are like those of wild carnivores or of dogs from antiquity. The teeth of wild carnivorous animals and those found in the fossils of the dog-like creatures of antiquity have far thicker and stronger enamel than those of our dogs today.

All hard natural bones are highly abrasive. If your dog is an avid chewer, natural bones may wear away his teeth

Rawhide treats are enjoyed by dogs. Owners should be wary since rawhide can tear off in large pieces and lodge in the dog's throat or cause intestinal blockage.

prematurely; hence, they then should be taken away from your dog when the teething purposes have been served. The badly worn, and usually painful, teeth of many mature dogs can be traced to excessive chewing on animal bones. Contrary to popular belief, knuckle bones that can be chewed up and swallowed by the dog provide little, if any, useable calcium or other nutrient. They do, however, disturb the digestion of most dogs and might cause them to vomit the nourishing food they really need.

Never give a dog your old shoe to chew on, even if you have removed all the nails or metal parts, such as lace grommets, buckles, metal arches, and so on. Rubber heels are especially dangerous, as the dog can bite off chunks, swallow them, and suffer from intestinal blockage as a result. Additionally, if the rubber should happen to have a nail imbedded in it that you cannot detect, this could pierce or tear the intestinal wall. There is always the possibility, too, that your dog may fail to differentiate between his shoe and yours and chew up a good pair while you're not looking. It is strongly recommended that you refrain from offering old shoes as chew toys, since there are much safer products available.

Rawhide treats are popular choices for dogs. Owners are advised to keep an eye on their dogs whenever they are playing with rawhide.

RAWHIDE CHEWS

The most popular material from which dog chews are made is the hide from cows, horses, and other animals. Most of these chews are made in foreign countries where the quality of the hide is not good enough for making leather. These foreign hides may contain lead, antibiotics, arsenic, or insecticides which might be detrimental to the health of your dog...or even your children. It is not impossible that a small child will start chewing on a piece of rawhide meant for the dog! Rawhide chews do not serve the primary chewing functions very well. They are also a bit messy when wet from mouthing, and most dogs chew them up rather rapidly. They have been considered safe for dogs until recently.

Rawhide is flavorful to dogs. They like it. Currently, some veterinarians have been attributing cases of acute constipation to large pieces of incompletely digested rawhide in the intestine. Basically it is good for them to chew on, but dogs think rawhide is food. They do not play with it nor do they use it as a pacifier to relieve doggie tension. They eat it as they would any other food. This is dangerous, for the hide is very difficult for dogs to digest and swallow, and many dogs choke on large particles of rawhide that become stuck in their throats. *Before you offer your dog rawhide chews, consult your veterinarian.* Vets have a lot of experience with canine chewing devices; ask them what they recommend.

NYLON CHEW DEVICES

The nylon bones, especially those with natural meat and bone flavor added, are probably the most complete, safe, and economical answer to the chewing need. Dogs cannot break them nor bite off sizeable chunks; hence, they are completely safe. And being longer lasting than other things offered for the purpose, they are very economical.

Hard chewing raises little bristle-like projections on the surface of the nylon bones to provide effective interim tooth cleaning and vigorous gum massage, much in the same way your toothbrush does it for you. The little projections are raked off and swallowed in the form of thin shavings, but the chemistry of the nylon is such that they break down in the stomach fluids and pass through without effect.

The toughness of the nylon provides the strong chewing resistance needed for important jaw exercise and effective help for the teething functions; however, there is no tooth wear because nylon is non-abrasive. Being inert, nylon does not

Annealed nylon and polyurethane chew toys are recommended by veterinarians as proven-safe and effective canine chew devices.

Polyurethane bones come in many colors and sizes. The Rainbows collection from Gumabone® adds flair to any dog's dental hygiene program.

support the growth of microorganisms, and it can be washed in soap and water or sterilized by boiling or in an autoclave.

There are a great variety of Nylabone® products available that veterinarians recommend as safe and healthy for your dog or puppy to chew on. These Nylabone® Pooch Pacifiers® usually don't splinter, chip, or break off in large chunks; instead, they are frizzled by the dog's chewing action, and this creates a toothbrush-like surface that cleanses the teeth and massages the gums. At the same time, these hard-nylon therapeutic devices channel doggie tension and chewing frustation into constructive rather than destructive behavior. The original nylon bone (Nylabone®) is not a toy and dogs use it only when in need of pacification. Keeping a bone in each of your dog's recreation rooms is the best method of providing the requisite pacification. Unfortunately, many nylon chew products have been copied. These inferior quality copies are sold in supermarkets and other chain stores. The really good products are sold only through veterinarians, pet shops, grooming salons and places where the sales people really know something about dogs. The good products have the flavor impregnated *into* the bone. This makes the taste last longer. The smell is undetectable to humans. The artificial bones which have a strong odor are poor-quality bones with the odor sprayed on to impress the dog owner (not the dog)! These heavily scented dog toys may impart the odor to your carpets or furniture if an odor-sprayed bone lies there wet from a dog's chewing on it.

FLOSS OR LOSS!

Most dentists relay that brushing daily is just not enough. In order to prevent unnecessary tooth loss, flossing is essential. For dogs, human dental floss is not the answer—however, canine dental devices are available. The Nylafloss® is a revolutionary product that is designed to save dogs teeth and keep them healthy. Even though your dogs won't believe you, Nylafloss® is not a toy but rather a most effective agent in removing destructive plaque between the teeth and *beneath* the gum line where gum disease begins. Gentle tugging is all that is necessary to activate the Nylafloss®. These 100% inert nylon products are guaranteed

to outlast rawhide chews by ten times and are available for sale at all pet shops.

THE IMPORTANCE OF PREVENTION

In order to get to the root of canine dentistry problems, it is important for owners to realize that no less than 75% of all canine dental health problems, serious enough to require a vet's assistance, and nearly 98% of all canine teeth lost are attributable to periodontal disease. Periodontal disease not only mars the teeth but also the gums and other buccal tissue in the mouth. Severe cases of periodontal disease involve resultant bacterial toxins which are absorbed into the blood

The Nylafloss® cannot cure tooth decay, but it is an optimum decay-prevention device. Make your dog's playtime a healthy time and invest in your pet's future.

stream and cause permanent damage to the heart and kidneys. In the infected mouth, teeth are loosened; tartar, unsightly and bad smelling, accumulates heavily; and the dog experiences a complete

The moderate calculus build-up on this dog's teeth reflects a certain neglect by the owner. Providing a safe chew item like the Gumabone® can help save your dog's teeth.

loss of appetite. Long-standing periodontitis can also manifest itself in simple symptoms such as diarrhea and vomiting.

Periodontal disease deserves the attention of every dog owner—a dog's teeth are extremely important to his ongoing health. The accumulation of plaque, food matter mixed with saliva attaching itself to the tooth surface, is a sure sign of potential bacteria build-up. As

toxic material gathers, the bone surrounding the teeth erodes. If plaque and calculus continue to reside without attention, bacteria-fighting cells will form residual pus at the root of the teeth, dividing the gum from the tooth. The debris is toxic and actually kills the buccal tissue. This is a most undesirable situation, as hardened dental calculus is one of the most direct causative agents of periodontitis.

In actuality, the disease is a result of a number of contributing factors. Old age, a diet comprised solely of soft or semi-soft foods, dental tartar, constant chewing of hair and even coprophagy (the eating of stool) are among the most common contributors.

Just as regular dental visits and brushing are necessary for humans, regular hygienic care and veterinary check-ups can help control tooth problems in canines. Involved and expensive routines can be performed on the affected, neglected mouth and teeth if decay has begun eroding the enamel and infecting the gums. Cleaning, polishing, and scaling are routine to remove calculus build-up.

Owners must claim responsibility for their dog's health, and tooth care is no small aspect of the care required. Daily brushing with a salt/baking soda solution is the best answer, but many owners find this tedious or just too difficult to perform. The simpler and more proven effective way to avoid, reduce, and fight periodontal disease and calculus build-up is giving the dog regular access to a thermoplastic polymer chew device. The Gumabone® products are the only scientifically proven line that offers the desired protection from calculus and tartar build-up.

Regular use of the Gumabone® chew products can significantly reduce plaque build-up.

CANINE DENTAL BREAKTHROUGH

The independent research of Dr. Andrew Duke, D.V.M., reveals that 70% of the dogs that regularly use Gumabone® experience a reduction of calculus build-up. This find is a breakthrough for the dog world, since the Gumabone® has already resided in the toy boxes of many dogs as their favorite play item. Little did owners know previously that their dogs were gaining entertainment and unparalleled dental treatment at the same time. Dr. Duke writes: "There is little debate left that dental calculus is an excellent indicator of periodontal health in the dog, just as it is in humans. "Calculus does not cause gingivitis and periodontitis, but the plaque and bacteria that cause periodontitis are

responsible for the mineral precipitation we know as 'calculus.' All veterinarians who have made a study of dogs' oral health have noticed the middle aged dog who actively chews with excellent gingival health. Many of these dogs that chew

Teeth of an infected dog showing little to no plaque accumulation after professional cleaning.

hard substances regularly wear the cusps down and even may expose the pulp cavity faster than secondary dentin can be formed. Often these "excellent chewers" are presented with slab fractures of the premolars or apical abcesses.

"The challenge then becomes to find a substance which is effective in removing calculus and plaque but does not wear the enamel excessively. In an attempt to duplicate the chewstuffs enjoyed by dogs in the wild, researchers have used bovine tracheas to demonstrate the inhibition of plaque and gingivitis. Very little else has been done in veterinary medicine to establish a scientific basis for evaluating chewstuffs.

"In the human field it is generally accepted (incorrectly) that fibrous foodstuffs and diet have no effect on oral health. This is a moot point since the practice of brushing is by far a more efficient technique of preventing plaque accumulation, calculus and periodontal disease. Studies in human subjects failed to find any benefits in eating apples, raw carrots, etc. If people are not allowed to brush, it is difficult to

The clean healthy teeth that are desired in dogs should inspire owners to work towards better dental hygiene.

Plaque is formed by the food debris and bacterial deposits left on teeth. Due to the high carbon dioxide and pH levels in the mouth, minerals precipitate quickly on the plaque to form calculus.

conduct clinical trials of more than one week.

"The increased awareness of animals' dental health of recent years has resulted in most veterinary practitioners' recommending some kind of chewstuff to their dog owners. To meet this market demand, there has been a stampede into the market by vendors ready to promote their products. The veterinarian is furnished no scientific data, but is asked to promote rawhide, bounce, and squeaky toys. How would our human colleagues handle this situation? Can Listerine® say that it prevents colds, but not support the claim? Can "Tartar Control Crest®" or "Colgate Tartar Control Formula®" be sold if it is not proven that it does in fact reduce tartar? Of course not.

"To this end, the following study was made.

"*Method:* Twenty dogs of different breeds and age were selected from a veterinary

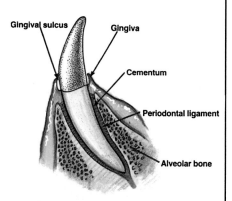

Gingival sulcus · Gingiva · Cementum · Periodontal ligament · Alveolar bone

Comparative look at healthy gums (above) and affected gums (below) *in a dog's mouth. Instinctively dogs need to massage their gums—and the Gumabone® can satisfy this doggie craving.*

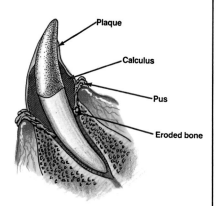

Plaque · Calculus · Pus · Eroded bone

practice's clientele. Although most were from multiple pet households, none were colony dogs. The owners were asked if they would allow their dogs to be anesthetized for two prophylactic cleanings which included root planing, polishing, and gingival debridement necessary to insure good oral hygiene.

"The dogs were divided into two groups of 10. Their teeth were cleaned and their calculus index converted to 0. One group was allowed only their normal dry commercial dog ration for 30 days. The other was allowed to have free choice access to Gumabone® products of the appropriate size.

"After 30 days, photoslides were made of the upper 3rd premolar, upper 4th premolar, and the lower 4th premolar on both sides of the dog's mouth. The dogs were again subjected to a prophylactic cleaning and the group reversed. After the second 30 days, photoslides were again made. A total of six teeth in each mouth were evaluated on each dog. This was 80 slides representing 240 teeth."

Fourteen out of 20 dogs (or 70%) experienced a reduction in calculus build-up by regularly using the Gumabone® product. These products are available in a variety of sizes (for different

Nylabone® and Gumabone® offer a new option for the choosy canine– chicken-flavored bones. Entertainment and pearly white teeth have never been better acquainted.

size dogs) and designed in interesting shapes: bones, balls, knots and rings (and even a tug toy). The entertainment value of the Gumabone® products is but an added advantage to the fighting of tooth decay and periodontitis. The products are ham-flavored and made of a thermoplastic polymer that is designed to outlast by ten times any rawhide, rubber or vinyl chew product, none of which can promise the proven benefit of the Gumabone®.

If your dog is able to chew apart a Gumabone®, it is probable that you provided him with a bone that is too small for him. Replace it with a larger one and the problem should not re-materialize. Economically, the Gumabone® is a smart choice, even without comparing it to the cost of extensive dental care.

Of course, nothing can *substitute* for periodic

In cases of bad neglect, scaling a dog's teeth can help to save or salvage affected teeth. Your veterinarian can perform this procedure.

professional attention to your dog's teeth and gums, no more than your toothbrush can replace your dentist. Have your dog's teeth cleaned by your veterinarian at least once a year—twice a year is better—

and he will be healthier, happier, and a far more pleasant companion.

Gumabones® are available through veterinarians and pet shops.

Canine tooth brushes are designed to allow access to the most hard-to-reach places in the canine mouth. Accustom your dog to brushing from puppyhood.

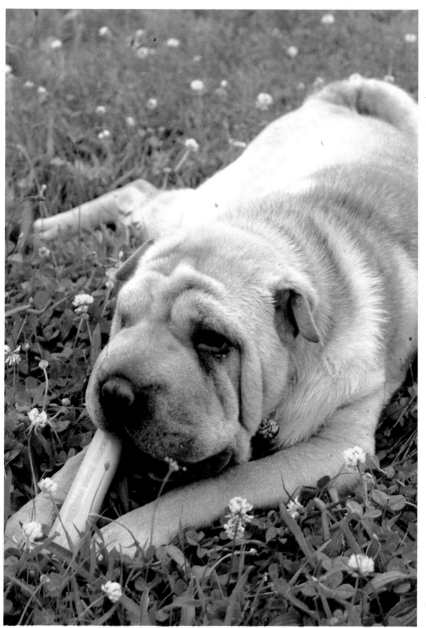

Clean teeth and good dental hygiene are easily accomplished with the right tools. This Shar-Pei has no worries with his favorite Nylabone.

Housebreaking and Training

HOUSEBREAKING

The new addition to your family may already have received some basic house training before his arrival in your home. If he has not, remember that a puppy will want to relieve himself about half a dozen times a day; it is up to you to specify where and when he should "do his business." Housebreaking is your first training concern and should begin the moment you bring the puppy home.

Ideally, puppies should be taken outdoors after meals, as a full stomach will exert pressure on the bladder and colon. What goes into the dog must eventually come out; the period

Four Paws Wee-Wee Pads are scientifically treated to attract puppies when nature calls. The plastic lining prevents damage to floors and carpets.

after his meal is the most natural and appropriate time. When he eliminates, he should be praised, for this will increase the likelihood of the same thing happening after every meal. He should also be encouraged to use the same area and will probably be attracted to it after frequent use.

Some veterinarians maintain that a puppy can learn to urinate and defecate on command, if properly trained. The advantage of this conditioning technique is that your pet will associate the act of elimination with a particular word of your choice rather than with a particular time or place which might not always be convenient or available. So whether you are visiting an unfamiliar place or don't want to go outside with your dog in sub-

zero temperatures, he will still be able to relieve himself when he hears the specific command word. Elimination will occur after this "trigger" phrase or word sets up a conditioned reflex in the dog, who will eliminate anything contained in his bladder or bowel upon hearing it. The shorter the word, the more you can repeat it and imprint it on your dog's memory.

Your chosen command word should be given simultaneously with the sphincter opening events in order to achieve perfect and rapid conditioning. This is why it is important to familiarize yourself with the tell-tale signs preceding your puppy's elimination process. Then you will be prepared to say the word at the crucial moment. There is usually a sense of

Crates assist in house-training the puppy. The dog's natural instinct is never to soil his sleeping area.

urgency on the dog's part; he may follow a sniffing and circling pattern which you will soon recognize. It is important to use the command in his usual area only when you know the puppy can eliminate, i.e., when his stomach or bladder is full. He will soon learn to associate the act with the word. One word of advice, however, if you plan to try out this method: never use the puppy's name or any other word which he might frequently hear about the house—you can imagine the result!

Finally, remember that any training takes time. Such a conditioned response can be obtained with intensive practice with any normal, healthy dog over six weeks of age. Even Pavlov's salivating dogs required fifty repetitions before the desired response was achieved. Patience and persistence will eventually produce results—do not lose heart!

Indoors, sheets of newspapers can be used to cover the specific area where your dog should relieve himself. These should be placed some distance away from his sleeping and feeding area, as a puppy

Although your Shar-Pei puppy is cute and innocent, without proper early training, he can grow to be an unmanageable and disobedient adult.

Puppies learn the ropes of canine behavior from a parent or older dog. If your adult dog has many bad habits, don't let him teach your new Shar-Pei pup any of his old tricks.

The choke collar and walking lead are commonly used in training.

will not urinate or defecate where he eats. When the newspapers are changed, the bottom papers should be placed on top of the new ones in order to reinforce the purpose of the papers by scent as well as by sight. The puppy should be praised during or immediately after he has made use of this particular part of the room. Each positive reinforcement increases the possibility of his using that area again.

When he arrives, it is advisable to limit the puppy to one room, usually the kitchen, as it most likely has a linoleum or easily washable floor surface. Given the run of the house, the sheer size of the place will seem overwhelming and confusing and he might leave his "signature" on your furniture or clothes! There will be time later to familiarize him gradually with his new surroundings.

PATIENCE, PERSISTENCE, AND PRAISE

As with a human baby, you must be patient, tolerant, and understanding of your pet's mistakes, making him feel loved and wanted, not rejected and isolated. You wouldn't hit a baby for soiling his diapers, as you would realize that he was not yet able to control his bowel movements; be as compassionate with your canine infant. Never rub his nose in his excreta. Never indulge in the common practice of punishing him with a rolled-up newspaper. Never hit a puppy with your hand. He will only become "hand-shy" and learn to fear you. Usually the punishment is meted out sometime after the offense and loses its efficacy, as the bewildered dog cannot connect the two events. Moreover, by association, he will soon learn to be afraid of you and anything to do with newspapers—including, perhaps, that area where he is

supposed to relieve himself!

Most puppies are eager to please. Praise, encouragement, and reward (particularly the food variety) will produce far better results than any scolding or physical punishment. Moreover, it is far better to dissuade your puppy from doing certain things, such as chewing on chair legs or other furniture, by making those objects particularly distasteful to him. Some pet shops stock bitter apple sprays or citronella compounds for application to furniture legs. These products are generally safer than old-fashioned home remedies. An owner may soon discover that application of these products may indeed make it seem as if

A simple dog collar or leash can be deceiving. Never be afraid to ask your pet shop proprietor exactly how a particular device is intended to work.

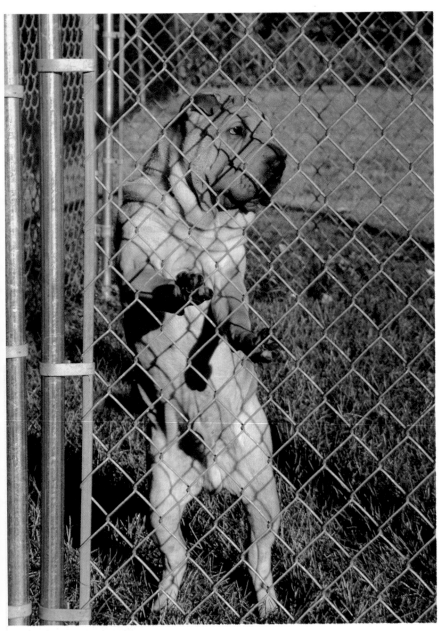

One alternative to a fenced-in yard is to provide your Shar-Pei with an outdoor exercise kennel. Owner, Alice S. Lawler.

the object itself was administering the punishment whenever he attempted to chew it. He probably wouldn't need a second reminder and your furniture will remain undamaged.

Remember that the reason a dog has housebreaking or behavior problems is because his owner has allowed them to develop. This is why you must begin as you intend to continue, letting your dog know what is acceptable and unacceptable behavior. It is also important that you be consistent in your demands; you cannot feed him from the dining room table one day and then punish him when he begs for food from your dinner guests.

TRAINING

You will want the newest member of your family to be welcomed by everyone; this will not happen if he urinates in every room of the house or barks all night! He needs training in the correct forms of behavior in this new human world. You cannot expect your puppy to become the perfect pet overnight. He needs your help in

Puppies are naturally clean animals. If your breeder has done his job, your new Shar-Pei should be nearly housebroken when you take him home.

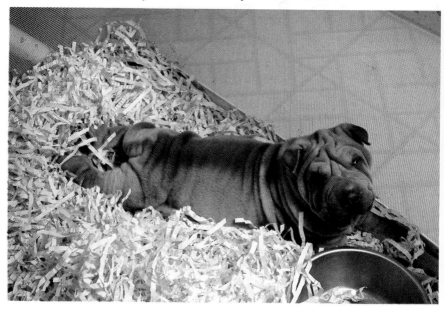

his socialization process. Training greatly facilitates and enhances the relationship of the dog to his owner and to the rest of society. A successfully trained dog can be taken anywhere and behave well with anyone. Indeed, it is that one crucial word—*training*—which can transform an aggressive animal into a peaceful, well-behaved pet. Now, how does this "transformation" take place?

WHEN AND HOW TO TRAIN

Like housebreaking, training should begin as soon as the puppy enters the house. The formal training sessions should be short but frequent, for example, ten to fifteen minute periods three times a day. These are much more effective than long, tiring sessions of half an hour which might soon become boring. You are building your relationship with your puppy during these times, so make them as enjoyable as possible. It is a good idea to have these sessions *before* the puppy's meal, not after it when he wouldn't feel like exerting himself; the dog will then associate something pleasurable with his training sessions and look forward to them.

A choke collar can be an effective training tool when properly used.

THE COLLAR AND LEASH

Your puppy should become used to a collar and leash as soon as possible. If he is very young, a thin, choke-chain collar can be used, but you will need a larger and heavier one for training when he is a little older. Remember to have his name and address on an identification tag attached to his collar, as you don't want to lose your pet if he should happen to leave your premises and explore the neighborhood!

Let the puppy wear his collar until he is used to how it feels. After a short time he will soon become accustomed to it and you can attach the leash. He might resist your attempts to lead him or simply sit down and refuse to budge. Fight him for a few minutes, tugging on the leash if necessary, then let him relax for the day. He won't be trained until he learns that he must obey the pull under any circumstance, but this will take a few sessions. Remember that a dog's period of concentration is short, so *little* and *often* is the wisest course of action—and patience is the password to success.

GIVING COMMANDS

When you begin giving your puppy simple commands, make them as short as possible and use the same word with the same meaning at all times, for example, "Heel," "Sit," and "Stay." You must be consistent; otherwise your puppy will become confused. The dog's name should prefix all commands to attract his attention. Do not become impatient with him however many times you have to repeat your command.

A good way to introduce the "Come" command is by calling the puppy when his meal is ready. Once this is learned, you can call your pet to you at will, always remembering to praise him for his prompt obedience. This "reward," or positive

Nylon and leather leads are the most popular with pet owners.

Although Shar-Pei puppies appear to be nearly identical, they each develop their own personalities, including likes and dislikes. A breeder can tell you much about the personality of each member of his litter.

reinforcement, is such a crucial part of training that a Director of the New York Academy of Dog Training constructed his whole teaching program upon the methods of "Love, Praise, and Reward." Incidentally, if you use the command "Come," use it every time. Don't switch to "Come here" or "Come boy," as this will only confuse your dog.

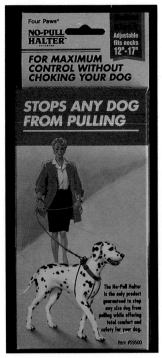
It is worth underlining the fact that punishment is an ineffective teaching technique. We have already seen this in housebreaking. For example, if your pup should run away, it would be senseless to beat him when he eventually returns; he would only connect the punishment with his return, not with running away! In addition, it is unwise to call him to you to punish him, as he will soon learn not to respond when you call his name.

SOME SPECIFIC COMMANDS

"Sit" This is one of the easiest and most useful commands for your dog to learn, so it is a good idea to begin with it. The only equipment required is a leash, a collar, and a few tasty tidbits. Take your dog out for some exercise before his meal. After about five minutes, call him to you, praise him when he arrives, and slip his collar on him. Hold the leash tightly in your right hand; this should force the dog's head up and focus his attention on you. As you say "Sit" in a loud, clear voice, with your left hand press steadily on his rump until he is in a sitting position. As soon as he is in the correct position, praise him and give him the tidbit you have in your hand. Now wait a few minutes to let him rest and repeat the routine. Through repetition, the dog soon associates the word with the act. Never make the lesson too long. Eventually your praise will be reward enough for your puppy. Other methods to teach this command exist, but this one, executed with care and moderation, has proven the most effective.

Great for the athletic dog and less-active owner are commercially designed retractable leads which give the dog much more freedom when exercising in an open field or cleared area.

"Sit-Stay/ Stay" To teach your pet to remain in one place or "stay" on your command, first of all order him to the sitting position at your side. Lower your left hand with the flat of your palm in front of his nose and your fingers pointing downwards. Hold the leash high and taut behind his head so that he cannot move. Speak the command "Sit-stay" and, as you are giving it, step in front of him. Repeat the command and tighten the leash so the animal cannot follow you. Walk completely around him, repeating the command and keeping him motionless by holding the leash at arm's length above him to check his movement. When he remains in this position for about fifteen seconds, you can begin the second part of the training. You will have to exchange the leash for a nylon cord or rope about twenty to thirty feet long. Repeat the whole routine from the beginning and be ready to prevent any movement towards you with a sharp "Sit-stay." Move around him in ever-widening circles until you are about fifteen feet away from him. If he still remains seated, you can pat yourself on the back! One useful thing to remember is that the dog makes associations with what you say, how you say it, and what you do while you are saying it. Give this command in a firm, clear tone of voice, perhaps using an admonishing forefinger raised, warning the dog to "stay."

"**Heel**" When you walk your dog, you should hold the leash firmly in your right hand. The dog should walk on your left so you have the leash crossing your body. This enables you to have greater control over the dog.

Let your dog lead you for the first few moments so that he fully understands that freedom can be his if he goes about it properly.

He already knows that when he wants to go outdoors the leash and collar are necessary, so he has respect for the leash. Now, if he starts to pull in one direction while walking, all you do is *stop walking*. He will walk a few steps and then find that he can't walk any further. He will then turn and look into your face. *This is the crucial point!* Just stand there for a moment and stare right back at him . . . now walk another ten feet and stop again. Again your dog will probably walk to the end of the leash, find he can't go any further, and turn around and look again. If he starts to pull and jerk, just stand there. After he quiets

It is important to allow your Shar-Pei time for play and exercise both before and after each training session. This will make training more enjoyable for owner and pet.

A collar and leash are essential tools for training as well as everyday activities.

down, bend down and comfort him, as he may be frightened. Keep up this training until he learns not to outwalk you.

Once the puppy obeys the pull of the leash, half of your training is accomplished. "Heeling" is a necessity for a well-behaved dog, so teach him to walk beside you, head even with your knee. Nothing looks sadder than a big dog taking his helpless owner for a walk. It is annoying to passers-by and other dog owners to have a large dog, however friendly, bear down on them and entangle dogs, people, and packages.

To teach your dog, start off walking briskly, saying "Heel" in a firm voice. Pull back with a sharp jerk if he lunges ahead, and if he lags repeat the command and tug on the leash, not allowing him to drag behind. After the dog has learned to heel at various speeds on leash, you can remove it and practice heeling free, but have it ready to snap on again as soon as he wanders.

"Come" Your dog has already learned to come to you when you call his name. Why? Because you only call him when his food is ready or when you wish to play with him or praise him. Outdoors such a response is more difficult to achieve, if he is happily playing by himself or with other dogs, so he must be trained to come to you when he is called. To teach him to come, let him reach the end of a long lead, then give the command, gently pulling him towards you at the same time. As soon as he associates the word *come* with the action of moving towards you, pull only when he does not respond immediately. As he starts to come, move back to make him learn that he must come from a distance as well as when he is close to you. Soon you may be able to practice without a leash, but if he is slow to come or actively disobedient, go to him and pull him toward you, repeating the command. Always remember to reward his successful completion of a task.

"Down" Teaching the "down" command ideally begins while your dog is still a pup. During puppyhood your dog frequently will lie down, as this position is one of the dog's most natural positions. Invest some time, and keep close watch over your pup. Each time he begins to lie, repeat in a low convincing tone the word "down." If for the first day of training, you concur a majority of the dog's sitting with your commands and continue with reinforcement and moderate praise your pup should conquer the "down" command in no time.

Teaching the "down" command to a mature dog likely will require more effort. Although the lying position is still natural to a dog, his being forced into it is not. Some dogs may react with fear, anger, or confusion. Others may accept the process and prove quick learners. Have your dog sit and face you. If he is responsive and congenial, gently take his paws, and slowly pull them towards you; give the "down" command as he approaches the proper position. Repeat several times: moderate reinforcement of this procedure should prove rewardingly successful.

For the dog that responds with anger or aggression, attach a lead (and a muzzle) and have the dog sit facing you at a close distance. There should be a J-loop formed by the lead. With moderate force, relative to the size and strength of your dog, step on the J-loop, forcing the dog down, while repeating the command "down" in a low forceful tone. When the dog is down, moderate praise should be given. If the dog proves responsive, you may attempt extending his legs to the "down" position—leaving the muzzle on, of course. Daily reinforcement of the training method will soon yield the desired results. The keys to remember are: patience, persistence, and praise.

Behavior Modification

"Problems with the Barking Dog" and "Aggressive Behavior and Dominance" are extracts from the veterinary monograph *Canine Behavior* (a compilation of columns from *Canine Practice,* a journal published by Veterinary Practice Publishing Company).

PROBLEMS WITH THE BARKING DOG

One of the most frequent complaints about canine behavior is barking. Aside from the biting dog, the barking dog is probably the pet peeve of many non-dog owners. I know of at least one city in which owners of dogs that bark excessively, and for which there are complaints on file, are required to take steps to eliminate the barking.

Canine practitioners are drawn into problems with barking when they are asked for their advice in helping an owner come up with a solution or, as a last resort, when they are requested to perform a debarking operation or even euthanasia. In this column I will deal with some of the factors that apparently cause dogs to bark and suggest some corrective approaches.

Barking is, of course, a natural response for many dogs. They have an inherited predisposition to bark as an alarm when other dogs or

Only in the most extreme situations may trainers recommend electric-shock collars for correcting a dog's misbehavior.

people approach their territory. Alarm barking makes many dogs valuable as household watchdogs and is not necessarily undesirable behavior. With a different vocal tone and pattern, dogs bark when they are playing with each other. On occasion dogs have a tendency to bark back at other dogs or join in with other barking dogs.

In addition to inherited barking tendencies, dogs can also learn to bark if the barking is followed, at least sometimes,

Shar-Pei come in many different solid colors. These members of Bruce Lee's Chinese Shar-Pei are examples of black, fawn and red.

by a reward. Thus dogs may bark when they wish to come in the house or to get out of a kennel. Some dogs are trained to bark upon hearing the command "speak" for a food reward.

One of the first approaches to take when discussing a barking problem is to determine if the behavior is a manifestation of a natural (inherited) tendency or is learned behavior which has been rewarded in the past.

Can Barking Be Extinguished? Extinction, as a way of eliminating a behavioral problem, may be considered when it is clear that the behavior has been learned and when one can identify the specific rewarding or reinforcing factors that maintain the behavior.

For example, the dog that barks upon hearing the command "speak" is periodically rewarded with food and praise. If a dog is never, ever given food or praise again when it barks after being told to "speak," it will eventually stop this type of barking. This is the process of extinction and it implies that the behavior must be repeated but never again rewarded.

A more practical example of the possible use of extinction would be in dealing with the dog that apparently barks because, at least occasionally, it is allowed in the house. By not allowing the dog in the house

Muzzles may prevent biting, but the root cause of biting must be extracted if the dog is to live as a trusted member of the human family.

until the barking has become very frequent and loud, the owners may have shaped the barking behavior to that which is the most objectionable. If the dog is never allowed in the house again when barking, the barking should eventually be extinguished—at least theoretically.

How Should Punishment Be Used? Sometimes it is not feasible to attempt to extinguish barking even if it seems to be the case that the behavior was learned. This brings up the advisability of punishment. Clients who seek advice in dealing with a barking problem may already have employed some type of punishment such as shouting at the dog or throwing something at it. That this type of punishment is ineffective is attested to by the fact that the client is seeking advice. By shouting at a dog or hitting, a person interferes with what effect the punishment may have on the behavior itself through the arousal of autonomic reactions and escape attempts or submissive responses by the dog.

The Water Bucket Approach
I am rather impressed by the ingenuity of some dog owners in coming up with ways to punish a dog for barking without being directly involved in administering the punishment. One such

Four Paws Quick Fit Muzzles are the most comfortable and humane muzzles for dogs. Allow dogs to drink water while wearing the muzzles. They are made of nylon and are completely washable.

The Shar-Pei has a very sensitive nose and if given the opportunity can excel in tracking.

Pet gates are used to confine a dog to certain areas of the house. The dog must learn to accept any such restrictions and not attempt to overcome them.

harried dog owner I talked to, who was also a veterinarian, was plagued by his dog's barking in the kennel commencing at about 1:30 a.m. every night. A platform to hold a bucket of water was constructed over the area of the kennel in which the dog usually chose to bark. Through a system of hinges, ropes, and pulleys, a mechanism was devised so that the dog owner could pull a rope from his bedroom window, dumping a bucket of water on the dog when he started to bark. The bucket was suspended such that once it was dumped, it

uprighted itself and the owner could fill it again remotely by turning on a garden hose. After two appropriate dunkings, the dog's barking behavior was apparently eliminated.

In advising a client on the type of punishment discussed above, keep in mind one important consideration. From the time the owner is ready to administer punishment for barking, every attempt should be made to punish all undesirable barking from that point on and not to allow excessively long periods of barking to go unpunished. Thus it may be necessary to keep a dog indoors when away unless the dog will be punished for barking when the owner is gone.

Alternative Responses

Barking dogs are, and probably always will be, one of the enduring problems of dog owners. Barking is relatively effortless, and it is such a natural response for many dogs that it is admittedly hard to eliminate with either punishment or a program of conditioning non-barking. In some instances it may be advisable to forget about eliminating barking and to suggest that the problem be dealt with by changing the circumstances which lead to barking. For example, a dog that barks continuously in the backyard while the owners are away may not bark if left in the house while they are gone. But the problem of keeping the dog in the house may be related to inadequate house training or the

Four Paws repellents are excellent training aids to keep dogs out of forbidden areas. Use indoors on furniture and rugs; outdoor formula for flowerbeds, shrubs and garbage cans.

The name Shar-Pei comes from Chinese meaning "sand-skin." Their coats are rough and prickly, which some have suggested was an effective method of protection for their dog-fighting ancestors.

dog's shedding hair or climbing onto the furniture. It may be easier to correct these latter behavioral problems than it is to change the barking behavior.

AGGRESSIVE BEHAVIOR AND DOMINANCE

Aggressiveness can have many causes. Determining what kind of aggression an animal is manifesting is a prerequisite to successful treatment of the behavior. A frequent problem that is presented to the practitioner is one of aggression related to dominance.

Dogs, which are social animals, have a hierarchal system of dominance within their pack. This predisposition to take a dominant or submissive position relative to fellow canines also occurs in relationship to people. Only in unusual situations would a submissive dog threaten a dominant animal, and almost never would it physically assault its superior. The dominant dog, however, frequently threatens submissive individuals to maintain its position. In a household setting, a person may be the object of threats, and when the person backs off, the dog's position is reassured. The aggressive behavior is also reinforced, and when behavior is reinforced it is likely to recur.

Owners must take an active part in shaping their dog's behavior. Providing a sensible chew device can help alleviate an animal's frustration and thereby eliminate some undersirable behavior. Once a dog has chewed the Gumabone® to this extent, it's time to buy a new one.

Case History The following is a typical case history of a dog presented for aggression stemming from dominance.

Max was a two-year-old intact male Cocker Spaniel. He had been acquired by Mr. Smith, one year prior to his owner's marriage, as a puppy. He liked and was well liked by both Mr. and Mrs. Smith. He frequently solicited and received attention from both people. However, several times over the last few months, Max had snapped at Mrs. Smith and repeatedly growled at her. A detailed anamnesis revealed that such incidents usually occurred in situations where the dog wanted his own way or did not want to be bothered. He would growl if asked to move off a chair or if persistently commanded to do a specific task. He growled if Mrs. Smith came between him and a young female Cocker Spaniel acquired a year ago. He also refused to let Mrs. Smith take anything from his possession. Max never showed any of these aggressive behaviors toward Mr. Smith or strangers. Admittedly he did not have much opportunity to demonstrate such behaviors toward strangers. A description of the dog's body and facial postures and circumstances under which the aggression occurred did not indicate that this was a case of fear-induced aggression, but rather one of

Treats can be effective in shaping behavior and establishing a rapport with your pet.

assertion of dominance.

Mrs. Smith's reaction to the aggression was always to retreat, and, hence, the dog was rewarded for his assertiveness. She had never physically disciplined the dog and was afraid to do so. To encourage her to physically take control of the dog would likely have resulted in her being bitten. The dominance-submissive

The large padded muzzle is characteristic of the Chinese Shar-Pei and is often referred to as a hippopotamus muzzle.

While crates may be used principally for sleeping and traveling, some owners might opt to employ a crate for disciplining a dog, rather like sending a naughty child to his room.

relationship had to be reversed in a more subtle manner.

Instructions to Client Mrs. Smith was instructed to avoid all situations which might evoke any aggressive signs from Max. This was to prevent any further reinforcement of his growling and threats.

Both she and her husband were not to indiscriminately pet or show affection towards the dog. For the time being, if Max

solicited attention from Mr. Smith, he was to ignore the dog. Mrs. Smith was to take advantage of Max's desire for attention by giving him a command which he had to obey before she praised and petted him. She was also to take advantage of high motivation levels for other activities whenever such situations arose. Max had to obey a command before she gave him anything—

before she petted him, before she let him out or in, etc.

Mrs. Smith also was to assume total care of the dog and become "the source of all good things in life" for Max. She was to feed him, take him on walks, play with him, etc.

Mrs. Smith also spent 5–10 minutes a day teaching Max simple parlor tricks and obedience responses for coveted food rewards as well as praise. These were entirely fun and play sessions—but within a few days the dog had acquired the habit of quickly responding to commands. And this habit transferred over to the non-game situations.

Results Within a few weeks, Max had ceased to growl and threaten Mrs. Smith in situations that he previously had. He would move out of her way or lie quietly when she would pass by him. She could order him off the furniture and handle the female Cocker Spaniel without eliciting threats from Max.

Mrs. Smith still felt that she would not be able to take the objects from Max's possession. Additional instructions were given to her. She then began placing a series of objects at progressively closer distances to the dog while the dog was in a sit-stay position. After she placed the object on the floor for a short time, she would pick it up. If the dog was still in a sit-stay (which it always was), he received a reward of cheese and verbal praise. Eventually the objects were to be placed and removed from directly in front of the dog. At first she was to use objects that the dog did not care much about and then progressively use more coveted items. This was what she was supposed to do, but before she actually had completed the program she called in excitedly to report that she had taken a piece of stolen food and a household ornament from Max's mouth. And he didn't even object! She said she had calmly told Max to sit. He did. He was so used to doing so, in the game and other situations, that the response was now automatic. She walked over, removed the item from his mouth, and praised him.

Mrs. Smith did resume the systematic presentation of objects and put the dog on an intermittent schedule of food and praise reinforcement during the practice sessions. Mr. Smith again began interacting with Max.

A progress check six months later indicated Max was still an obedient dog and had definitely assumed a submissive position relative to both of his owners. The dominance hierarchy between Max and Mrs. Smith had been reversed *without resorting to any physical punishment.* Mrs. Smith was instructed to reinforce her dominance position by frequently giving Max a command and reinforcing him for the appropriate response.

Summary The essential elements in treatment of such cases are as follows. First, of course, there must be a correct diagnosis of what kind of aggressive behavior is occurring. During the course of treatment, the submissive person(s) should avoid all situations that might evoke an aggressive attitude by the dog. All other family members should totally ignore the dog during the treatment interim. The person most dominated by the dog should take over complete care of the dog in addition to spending 5–10 minutes a day teaching the dog tricks or simple obedience commands (sit-stay is a useful one to gain control of the dog in subsequent circumstances). These should be fun-and-games situations. Food rewards are highly recommended in addition to simple praise.

The person submissive to the dog should take the opportunity to give the dog a command, which must be obeyed, before doing anything pleasant for the dog.

Four Paws offers Bitter Lime in two ways. A pump spray to stop fur biting and a gel to stop chewing of furniture. Both are safe and non-toxic.

It must be emphasized to the owner that no guarantee can be made that the dog will never threaten or be aggressive again. What is being done, as with all other aggression cases, is an attempt to reduce the likelihood, incidence, and intensity of occurrence of the aggressive behavior.

Old discardable shoes should not be included in the dog's toy box. Such items are dangerous to a puppy or an adult dog.

DESTRUCTIVE TENDENCIES

It is ironical but true that a dog's destructive behavior in the home may be proof of his love for his owner. He may be trying to get more attention from his owner or, in other cases, may be expressing his frustration at his owner's absence. An abundance of unused energy may also contribute to a dog's destructive behavior, and therefore the owner should ensure that his dog has, at least, twenty minutes of vigorous exercise a day.

As a dog's destructive tendencies may stem from his desire to get more attention from his owner, the latter should devote specific periods each day to his dog when he is actively interacting with him. Such a period should contain practice obedience techniques during which the owner can reward the dog with his favorite food as well as praise and affection.

Planned departure conditioning is one specific technique which has been used to solve the problem of destructive tendencies in a puppy. It eventually ensures the dog's good behavior during the owner's absence. A series of short departures, which are identical to real departures, should condition the dog to behave well in the owner's absence. How is this to be achieved? Initially, the departures are so short (2–5 minutes) that the dog has no opportunity to be destructive.

The dog is always rewarded for having been good when the owner returns. Gradually the duration of the departures is increased. The departure time is also varied so that the dog does not know when the owner is going to return. Since a different kind of behavior is now expected, it is best if a new stimulus or "atmosphere" is introduced into the training sessions to permit the dog to distinguish these departures as different from previous departures when he was destructive.

This new stimulus could be the sound of the radio or television. The association which the dog will develop is that whenever the "signal" or "stimulus" is on, the owner will return in an unknown period of time and, if the dog has not been destructive, he will be rewarded. As with the daily owner-dog interaction, the food reward is especially useful.

If the dog misbehaves during his owner's absence, the owner should speak sternly to him and isolate him from social contact for at least thirty minutes. (Puppies hate to be ignored.)

Then the owner should conduct another departure of a shorter time and generously reward good behavior when he returns. The owner should progress slowly enough in the program so that once the departure has been initiated, the dog is never given an opportunity to make a mistake.

If planned departures are working satisfactorily, the departure time

There is a wide variety of collars and harnesses available to the dog owner. Talk with your pet shop proprietor to determine which one best satisfies your needs.

may gradually be extended to several hours. To reduce the dog's anxiety when left alone, he should be given a "safety valve" such as the indestructible Nylabone® to play with and chew on.

Health Care

From the moment you purchase your puppy, the most important person in both your lives becomes your veterinarian. His professional advice and treatment will ensure the good health of your pet. The vet is the first person to call when illness or accidents occur. Do *not* try to be your own veterinarian or apply human remedies to canine diseases. However, just as you would keep a first aid kit handy for minor injuries sustained by members of your family at home, so you should keep a similar kit prepared for your pet.

First aid for your dog would consist of stopping any bleeding, cleaning the wound, and preventing infection. Thus your kit might contain medicated powder, gauze bandages, and adhesive tape to be used in case of cuts. If the cut is deep and bleeding profusely, the bandage should be applied very tightly to help in the formation of a clot. A tight bandage should not be kept in place longer than necessary, so take your pet to the veterinarian immediately.

Walking or running on a cut pad prevents the cut from healing. Proper suturing of the cut and regular changing of the bandages should have your pet's wound healed in a week to ten

Bandaging a minor cut on the paw pad is one of many basic first-aid techniques that the dog owner should learn. Thoroughly clean the injury with peroxide and apply an antibiotic. Then place the injured pad in sterile gauze, secure with first-aid tape, and replace daily.

days. A minor cut should be covered with a light bandage, for you want as much air as possible to reach the wound. Do not apply wads of cotton to a wound, as they will stick to the area and may cause contamination.

You should also keep some hydrogen peroxide available, as it is useful in cleaning wounds and is also one of the best and simplest emetics known. Cotton applicator swabs are useful for applying ointment or removing debris from the eyes. A pair of tweezers should also be kept handy for removing foreign bodies from the dog's neck, head or body.

Nearly everything a dog might contract in the way of sickness has basically the same set of symptoms: loss of appetite, diarrhea, dull eyes, dull coat, warm and/or runny nose, and a high temperature. Therefore, it is most important to take his temperature at the first sign of illness. To do this, you will need a rectal thermometer which should be lubricated with petroleum jelly. Carefully insert it into the rectum, holding it in place for at least two minutes. It must be held firmly; otherwise there is the danger of its being sucked up into the rectum or slipping out, thus giving an inaccurate reading. The normal temperature for a dog is between 101° and 102.5°F. If your pet is

Four Paws Crystal Eye is a safe product for the removal of ugly tear stains.

seriously ill or injured in an accident, your veterinarian will advise you what to do before he arrives.

SWALLOWING FOREIGN OBJECTS

Most of us have had experience with a child swallowing a foreign object. Usually it is a small coin; occasionally it may be a fruit pit or something more dangerous. Dogs, *as a general rule,* will not swallow anything which isn't edible. There are, however, many dogs that swallow pebbles or small shiny objects such as pins, coins, and bits of cloth and plastic. This is especially true of dogs that are offered so-called "chew toys."

Chew toys are available in many sizes, shapes, colors and materials. Some even have whistles which sound when the dog's owner plays with it or when the dog chomps on it quickly. Most dogs attack the whistle first, doing everything possible to make it stop squeaking. Obviously, if the whistle is made of metal, a dog

The contents of a full ashtray if consumed by the curious dog may induce nicotine poisoning. Pet owners must dog-proof their home for the safety of their animals.

When emergencies occur, being prepared pays off. A first-aid kit should be accessible and always well stocked with medical accessories and supplies.

can injure its mouth, teeth, or tongue. Therefore, *never* buy a "squeak toy" made with a metal whistle.

Other chew toys are made of vinyl, a cheap plastic which is soft to the touch and pliable. Most of the cute little toys that are figures of animals or people are made of this cheap plastic. They are sometimes hand-painted in countries where the cost of such labor is low. Not only is the paint used dangerous to dogs, because of the lead content, but the vinyl tears easily and is usually destroyed by the dog during the first hour. Small bits of vinyl

may be ingested and cause blockage of the intestines. You are, therefore, reminded of these things before you buy anything vinyl for your dog!

Very inexpensive dog toys, usually found in supermarkets and other low-price venues, may be made of polyethylene. These are to be avoided completely, as this cheap plastic is, for some odd reason, attractive to dogs. Dogs destroy the toy in minutes and sometimes swallow the indigestible bits and pieces that come off. Most pet shops carry only safe toys.

WHAT TOYS ARE SAFE FOR DOGS?

Hard Rubber Toys made of hard rubber are usually safe for dogs, providing the toy is made of 100% hard rubber and not a compound of rubber and other materials. The rubber must be "virgin" and not re-ground from old tires, tubes, and other scrap rubber products. The main problem with rubber, even 100% virgin rubber, is that it oxidizes quickly, especially when subjected to the ultraviolet rays of the sun and a dog's saliva. The rubber then tends to be brittle, to crack, to dust off, and to be extremely dangerous to dogs that like swallowing things.

Nylon Toys Toys made of nylon could well be the safest of all toys, *providing the nylon is annealed.* Nylon that is not annealed is very fragile, and if you smash it against a hard surface, it might shatter like glass. The same is true when the weather is cold and the nylon drops below freezing. Thus far there is only one line of dog toys that is made of annealed virgin nylon—Nylabone®. These toys not only are annealed but they are flavored and scented. The flavors and scents, such as hambone, are undetectable by humans, but dogs seem to find them attractive.

Some nylon bones have the

The Plaque Attacker® is a Dental Ball™, not just a plaything, designed to reduce plaque and tartar by use of its revolutionary "dental tips."

flavor sprayed on them or molded into them. These cheaper bones are easy to detect—just smell them. If you discern an odor, you know they are poorly made. The main problem with the nylon toys that have an odor is that they are not annealed and they "smell up" the house or car. The dog's saliva dilutes the odor of the bone, and when he drops it on your rug, this odor attaches itself to the rug and is quite difficult to remove.

The Puppy Bone® by Nylabone® is multi-purpose: designed for teething, chew-pacification, teeth-cleaning and the elimination of behavioral problems before they become habitual.

Gumabone® is available in different sizes and shapes. These are probably the most popular of all chew toys because dogs love them.

Annealed nylon may be the best there is, but it is not 100% safe. The Nylabone® dog chews are really meant to be Pooch Pacifiers®. This trade name indicates the effect intended for the dog, which is to relieve the tension in your excited puppy or anxious adult dog. Instead of chewing up the furniture or some other object, he chews up his Nylabone® instead. Many dogs ignore the Nylabone® for weeks, suddenly attacking it when they have to relieve their doggie tensions.

The Nylabone® is designed for the most aggressive chewers. Even so, owners should be wary that some dogs may have jaws strong enough to chomp off a piece of Nylabone®, but this is extremely rare. *One word of caution:* the Nylabone® should be replaced when the dog has chewed down the knuckle. Most dogs slowly scrape off small slivers of nylon which pass harmlessly through their digestive tract. The resultant frizzled bone actually becomes a toothbrush.

One of the great characteristics of nylon bones is that they can be boiled and sterilized. If a dog loses interest in his Nylabone®, or it is too hard for him to chew due to his age and the condition of his teeth, you can cook it in some chicken or beef broth, allowing it to boil for 30 minutes. Let it cool down normally. It will then be perfectly sterile and re-flavored for the next dog. *Don't try this with plastic bones, as they will melt and ruin your pot.*

Polyurethane Toys Because polyurethane bones such as the Gumabone® are constructed of

Plaque Attacker™ Dental Bones from Gumabone® are designed for maximum tartar reduction for the aggressive chewer.

the strongest *flexible* materials known, some dogs (and their owners) actually prefer them to the traditional nylon bones. There are several brands on the market: ignore the ones which have scents that you can discern. Some of the scented polyurethane bones have an unbearable odor after the scent has rubbed off the bone and onto your rug or car seat. Again, look for the better-quality polyurethane toy. Gumabone® is a flexible material, the same as used for making artificial hearts and the bumpers on automobiles, thus it is strong and stable. It is not as strong as Nylabone®, but many dogs like it because it is soft.

If your dog is soft-mouthed and a less aggressive, more playful chewer, he will love the great taste and fun feel of the Gumabone® products.

The most popular of the Gumabone® products made in polyurethane are the tug toys, knots, balls, and Frisbee® flying discs. These items are almost clear in color, have the decided advantage of lasting a long time, and are useful in providing exercise for both a dog and his master or mistress.

Made of a more flexible material than nylon, Gumabone® devices often are more appealling to dogs.

Gumabone® has also introduced new spiral-shaped dental devices under the name Plaque Attacker®. These unique products are fast becoming standards for all aggressive chewers. The Plaque Attacker Dental Device® comes in four fun sizes and each is designed to maximize gum and teeth massage through its upraised "dental tips," which pimple the surface of the toy. Similarly, the Plaque Attacker Dental Ball® ensures a reduction in plaque and tartar. This one-of-a-kind product provides hours of fun for a dog. It bounces erratically and proves to be the most exciting of all polyurethane toys. All Plaque Attacker® products are patented and scented with hambone to make them even more enticing for the dog. Clinical findings

The Plaque Attacker™ Dental Ball® is a unique and challenging toy for dogs big and small.

support the assertion that a significant reduction in calculus accompanies use of the Gumbone® products.

Whatever dog toy you buy, be sure it is high quality. Pet shops and certain supermarkets, as a rule, always carry the better-quality toys. Of course there may be exceptions, but you are best advised to ask your local pet shop operator—or even your veterinarian—what toys are suitable for *your* dog.

In conclusion, if your dog is a swallower of foreign objects, don't give him anything cheap to chew on. If he swallows a coin, you can hardly blame the Treasury! Unless your dog is carefully supervised, use only the largest size Nylabone® and Gumabone®, and replace them as soon as the dog chews down the knuckles. *Do not let the dog take the Nylabone® outdoors.* First of all he can hide and bury it, digging it up when his tensions rise. Then, too, all nylon becomes more brittle when it freezes, even Nylabone®.

IF YOUR PET SWALLOWS POISON

A poisoned dog must be treated instantly; any delay could cause his death. Different poisons act in different ways and require different treatments. If you know the dog has swallowed an acid, alkali, gasoline, or kerosene, do not induce vomiting. Give milk to dilute the poison and rush him to the vet. If you can find the bottle or container of poison, check the label to see if there is a recommended antidote. If not, try to induce vomiting by giving him a mixture of hydrogen peroxide and water. Mix the regular drugstore strength of hydrogen peroxide (3%) with an equal part of water, but do not attempt to

Four Paws offers three pleasantly scented colognes that can be used in between baths to freshen up pets.

pour it down your dog's throat, as that could cause inhalation pneumonia. Instead, simply pull the dog's lips away from the side of his mouth, making a pocket for depositing the liquid. Use at least a tablespoonful of the mixture for every ten pounds of your dog's weight. He will vomit in about two minutes. When his stomach has settled, give him a teaspoonful of Epsom salts in a little water to empty the intestine quickly. The hydrogen peroxide, on ingestion, becomes oxygen and water and

is harmless to your dog; it is the best antidote for phosphorus, which is often used in rat poisons. After you have administered this emergency treatment to your pet and his stomach and bowels have been emptied, rush him to your veterinarian for further care.

DANGER IN THE HOME

There are numerous household products that can prove fatal if ingested by your pet. These include rat poison,

Wasps can be harmful to dogs and humans alike. Paper wasps often build their nests close to the ground, where a dog may happen to visit.

antifreeze, boric acid, hand soap, detergents, insecticides, mothballs, household cleansers, bleaches, de-icers, polishes and disinfectants, paint and varnish removers, acetone, turpentine, and even health and beauty aids if ingested in large enough quantities. A word to the wise should be sufficient: what you would keep locked away from your two-year-old child should also be kept hidden from your pet.

There is another danger lurking within the home among the household plants, which are almost all poisonous, even if swallowed in small quantities. There are hundreds of poisonous plants around us, among which are: ivy leaves, cyclamen, lily of the valley, rhododendrons, tulip bulbs, azalea, wisteria, poinsettia leaves, mistletoe, daffodils, delphiniums, foxglove leaves, the jimson weed—we cannot name them all. Rhubarb leaves, for example, either raw or cooked, can cause death or violent convulsions. Peach, elderberry, and cherry trees can cause cyanide poisoning if their bark is consumed.

There are also many insects that can be poisonous to dogs

such as spiders, bees, wasps, and some flies. A few toads and frogs exude a fluid that can make a dog foam at the mouth—and even kill him—if he bites too hard!

There have been cases of dogs suffering nicotine poisoning by consuming the contents of full ashtrays which thoughtless smokers have left on the coffee table. Also, do not leave nails, staples, pins, or other sharp objects lying around. Likewise, don't let your puppy play with plastic bags which could suffocate him. Unplug, remove, or cover any electrical cords or wires near your dog. Chewing live wires could lead to severe

mouth burns or death. Remember that an ounce of prevention is worth a pound of cure: keep all potentially dangerous objects out of your pet's reach.

VEHICLE TRAVEL SAFETY

A dog should never be left alone in a car. It takes only a few minutes for the heat to become unbearable in the summer, and to drop to freezing in the winter.

A dog traveling in a car or truck should be well behaved. An undisciplined dog can be deadly in a moving vehicle. The dog should be trained to lie on the back seat of the vehicle. Allowing your dog to stick its head out of

Car safety is a serious matter. When a dog is traveling by auto, specially designed seat belts (or the dog's crate) are the safest route.

Four Paws Pet Safety Sitter is designed to protect pets from injury by securing them in place and preventing them from disturbing drivers and passengers.

the window is unwise. The dog may jump or it may get something in its eye. Some manufacturers sell seat belts and car seats designed for dogs.

Traveling with your dog in the back of your pick-up truck is an unacceptable notion and dangerous to all involved.

PROTECT YOURSELF FIRST

In almost all first aid situations, the dog is in pain. He may indeed be in shock and not appear to be suffering, until you move him. Then he may bite your hand or resist being helped at all. So if you want to help your dog, help yourself first by tying his mouth closed. To do this, use a piece of strong cloth four inches wide and three feet long, depending on the size of the dog. Make a loop in the middle of the strip and slip it over his nose with the knot under his chin and over the bony part of his nose. Pull it tight and bring the ends back around his head behind the ears and tie it tightly, ending with a bow knot for quick, easy release. Now you can handle the dog safely. As a dog perspires through his tongue, do not leave the "emergency muzzle" on any longer than necessary.

ADMINISTERING MEDICINE

When you are giving liquid medicine to your dog, it is a good idea to pull the lips away from the side of the mouth, form a lip pocket, and let the liquid trickle past the tongue. Remain at his side, never in front of the dog, as he may cough and spray you with the liquid. Moreover, you must never pour liquid medicine while the victim's tongue is drawn out, as inhalation pneumonia could be the disastrous result.

Medicine in pill form is best administered by forcing the dog's mouth open, holding his head back, and placing the capsule as far back on his tongue as you can reach. To do this: put the palm of your hand over the dog's muzzle (his foreface) with your fingers on one side of his jaw, your thumb on the other. Press his lips hard against his teeth while using your other hand to pull down his lower jaw. With your two fingers, try to put the pill

as far back on the dog's tongue as you can reach. Keep his mouth and nostrils closed and he should be forced to swallow the medicine. As the dog will not be feeling well, stroke his neck to comfort him and to help him swallow his medicine more easily. Do keep an eye on him for a few moments afterward, however, to make certain that he does not spit it out.

IN CASE OF AN ACCIDENT

It is often difficult for you to assess the dog's injuries after a road accident. He may appear normal, but there might be

Choose from a variety of ear care products from Four Paws from cleaners to remedies for proper ear hygiene.

internal hemorrhaging. A vital organ could be damaged or ribs broken. Keep the dog as quiet and warm as possible; cover him with blankets or your coat to let his own body heat build up. Signs of shock are a rapid and weak pulse, glassy-eyed appearance, subnormal temperature, and slow capillary refill time. To determine the last symptom, press firmly against the dog's gums until they turn white. Release and count the number of seconds until the gums return to their normal color. If it is more than 2–3 seconds, the dog may be going into shock. Failure to return to the reddish pink color indicates that the dog may be in serious trouble and needs immediate assistance.

If artificial respiration is required, first open the dog's mouth and check for obstructions; extend his tongue and examine the pharynx. Clear his mouth of mucus and blood and hold the mouth slightly open. Mouth-to-mouth resuscitation involves holding the dog's tongue to the bottom of his mouth with one hand and sealing his nostrils with the other while you blow into his mouth. Watch for his chest to rise with each inflation. Repeat every 5–6 seconds, the equivalent of 10–12 breaths a minute.

If the veterinarian cannot come to you, try to improvise a stretcher to take the dog to him. To carry a puppy, wrap him in a blanket that has been folded into several thicknesses. If he is in shock, it is better to pick him up by holding one hand under his chest, the other under the hindquarters. This will keep him stretched out.

It is always better to roll an injured dog than to try and lift him. If you find him lying beside the road after a car accident, apply a muzzle even if you have to use someone's necktie to make one. Send someone for a blanket and roll him gently onto it. Two people, one on each side, can make a stretcher out of the blanket and move the dog easily.

If no blanket is available and the injured dog must be moved, try to keep him as flat as possible. So many dogs' backs are broken in car accidents that one must first consider that possibility. However, if he can move his hind legs or tail, his spine is probably not broken. Get medical assistance for him immediately.

It should be mentioned that unfortunate car accidents, which can maim or kill your dog, can be avoided if he is confined at all times either indoors or, if out-of-doors, in a fenced-in yard or some other protective enclosure. *Never* allow your dog to roam free; even a well-trained dog may, for some unknown reason,

VACCINATION SCHEDULE

Age	Vaccination
6-8 weeks	Initial canine distemper, canine hepatitis, tracheobronchitis, canine parvovirus, as well as initial leptospirosis vaccination.
10-12 weeks	Second vaccination for all given at 6-8 weeks. Initial rabies and initial Lyme disease to be given at this time.
14-16 weeks	Third vaccination for all given at 6-8 and 10-12 weeks.Re-vaccinate annually, hereafter. Second rabies and second Lyme disease to be given at this time, and then re-vaccinated annually.

Vaccination schedules should be confirmed with your vet.

dart into the street—and the result could be tragic.

If you need to walk your dog, leash him first so that he will be protected from moving vehicles.

PROTECTING YOUR PET

It is important to watch for any tell-tale signs of illness so that you can spare your pet any unnecessary suffering. Your dog's eyes, for example, should normally be bright and alert, so if the haw is bloodshot or partially covers the eye, it may be a sign of illness or irritation. If your dog has matter in the corners of his eyes, bathe them with a mild eye wash; obtain ointment or eye drops from your veterinarian to treat a chronic condition.

If your dog seems to have something wrong with his ears which causes him to scratch at them or shake his head, cautiously probe the ear with a cotton swab. An accumulation of wax will probably work itself out. Dirt or dried blood, however, is indicative of ear mites or infection and should be treated immediately. Sore ears in the summer, due to insect bites, should be washed with mild soap and water, then covered with a soothing ointment and wrapped in gauze if necessary. Keep your

Mosquitoes are the vectors of disease; although males like this one do not bite, females can transmit heartworm and other diseases to dogs.

pet away from insects until his ears heal, even if this means confining him indoors.

INOCULATIONS

Periodic check-ups by your veterinarian throughout your puppy's life are good health insurance. The person from whom your puppy was purchased should tell you what inoculations your puppy has had and when the next visit to the vet is necessary. You must make certain that your puppy has been vaccinated against the following infectious canine diseases:

distemper, canine hepatitis, leptospirosis, rabies, parvovirus, and parainfluenza. Annual "boosters" thereafter provide inexpensive protection for your dog against such serious diseases. Puppies should also be checked for worms at an early age.

DISTEMPER

Young dogs are most susceptible to distemper, although it may affect dogs of all ages. Some signs of the disease are loss of appetite, depression, chills, and fever, as well as a watery discharge from the eyes and nose. Unless treated promptly, the disease goes into advanced stages with infections of the lungs, intestines, and nervous system. Dogs that recover may be impaired with paralysis, convulsions, a twitch, or some other defect, usually spastic in nature. Early inoculations in puppyhood should be followed by an annual booster to help protect against this disease.

CANINE HEPATITIS
The signs of hepatitis are drowsiness, loss of appetite, high temperature, and great thirst. These signs may be accompanied by swellings of the head, neck, and abdomen. Vomiting may also occur. This disease strikes quickly, and death may occur in only a few hours. An annual booster shot is

needed after the initial series of puppy shots.

LEPTOSPIROSIS
Infection caused by either of two serovars, *canicola* or *copehageni,* is usually begun by the dog's licking substances contaminated by the urine or feces of infected animals. Brown rats are the main carriers of *copehageni.* The signs are weakness, vomiting, and a

Biting bugs not only have a painful bite but also carry blood parasites.

yellowish discoloration of the jaws, teeth, and tongue, caused by an inflammation of the kidneys. A veterinarian can administer the bacterins to protect your dog from this disease. The frequency of the doses is determined by the risk factor involved.

RABIES

This disease of the dog's central nervous system spreads by infectious saliva, which is transmitted by the bite of an infected animal. Of the two main classes of signs, the first is "furious rabies," in which the dog shows a period of melancholy or depression, then irritation, and finally paralysis. The first period can be from a few hours to several days, and during this time the dog is cross and will change his position often, lose his appetite, begin to lick, and bite or swallow foreign objects. During this phase the dog is spasmodically wild and has impulses to run away. The dog acts fearless and bites everything in sight. If he is caged or confined, he will fight at the bars and possibly break teeth or fracture his jaw. His bark becomes a peculiar howl. In the final stage, the animal's lower jaw becomes paralyzed and

Heartworm life cycle: a carrier mosquito bites a dog and deposits microfilariae, which travel through the dog's bloodstream, lodging in the heart to reproduce. The carrier dog is later bitten by an uninfected mosquito, which becomes infected, and bites and infects another dog...

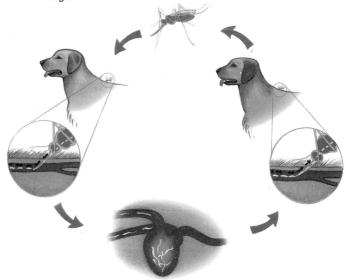

hangs down. He then walks with a stagger, and saliva drips from his mouth. About four to eight days after the onset of paralysis, the dog dies.

The second class of symptoms is referred to as "dumb rabies" and is characterized by the dog's walking in a bearlike manner with his head down. The lower jaw is paralyzed and the dog is unable to bite. It appears as if he has a bone caught in his throat.

If a dog is bitten by a rabid animal, he probably can be saved if he is taken to a veterinarian in time for a series of injections. After the signs appear, however, no cure is possible. The local health department must be notified in the case of a rabid dog, for he is a danger to all who come near him. As with the other shots each year, an annual rabies inoculation is very important. In many areas, the administration of rabies vaccines for dogs is required by law.

PARVOVIRUS

This relatively new virus is a contagious disease that has spread in almost epidemic proportions throughout certain sections of the United States. It has also appeared in Australia, Canada, and Europe. Canine parvovirus attacks the intestinal tract, white blood cells, and heart

Lice are not a common problem in dogs and usually only infest dogs that are poorly cared for. Proper care of your dog will prevent lice infestation.

muscle. It is believed to spread through dog-to-dog contact, and the specific course of infection seems to come from fecal matter of infected dogs. Overcoming parvovirus is difficult, for it is capable of existing in the environment for many months under varying conditions and temperatures, and it can be transmitted from place to place

Four Paws Protector Flea & Tick Spray offers a quick kill and will repel fleas for up to 14 days. Super Fly Repellent repels flies and mosquitoes, which are known to transmit heartworm.

streaked. Because of the vomiting and severe diarrhea, the dog that has contracted the disease will dehydrate quickly. Depression and loss of appetite, as well as a rise in temperature, can accompany the other symptoms. Death caused by this disease usually occurs within 48 to 72 hours following the appearance of the symptoms. Puppies are hardest hit, and the virus is fatal to 75 percent of puppies that contract it. Death in puppies can be within two days of the onset of the illness.

A series of shots administered by a veterinarian is the best preventive measure for canine parvovirus. It is also important to disinfect the area where the dog is housed by using one part sodium hypochlorite solution (household bleach) to 30 parts of water and to keep the dog from coming into contact with the fecal matter of other dogs.

on the hair and feet of infected dogs, as well as on the clothes and shoes of people.

Vomiting and severe diarrhea, which will appear within five to seven days after the animal has been exposed to the virus, are the initial signs of this disease. At the onset of illness, feces will be light gray or yellow-gray in color, and the urine might be blood-

LYME DISEASE

Known as a bacterial infection, Lyme disease is transmitted by ticks infected with a spirochete known as *Borrelia burgdorferi*. The disease is most often acquired by the parasitic bite of an infected deer tick, *Ixodes dammini*. While the range of symptoms is broad, common warning signs include: rash beginning at the bite and soon extending in a bullseye-targetlike fashion; chills, fever, lack of balance, lethargy, and stiffness; swelling and pain, especially in the joints, possibly leading to arthritis or arthritic conditions; heart problems, weak limbs, facial paralysis, and lack of tactile sensation.

Concerned dog owners, especially those living in the United States, should contact a veterinarian to discuss Lyme disease. A vaccination has been developed and is routinely administered to puppies twice before the 16th week, and then repeated annually.

PARAINFLUENZA

Parainfluenza, or infectious canine tracheobronchitis, is commonly known as "kennel cough." It is highly contagious, affects the upper respiratory system, and is spread through direct or indirect contact with already diseased dogs. It will readily infect dogs of all ages that have not been vaccinated or that were previously infected. While this condition is definitely one of the serious diseases in dogs, it is self-limiting, usually lasting only two to four weeks. The symptoms are high fever and intense, harsh coughing that brings up mucus. As long as

The fraternity of internal parasites and their eggs: whipworms, hookworms, roundworms and tapeworms.

your pet sees your veterinarian immediately, the chances for his complete recovery are excellent.

EXTERNAL PARASITES

A parasite is an animal that lives in or on an organism of another species, known as the host, without contributing to the well-being of the host. The majority of dogs' skin problems are parasitic in nature and an estimated 90% of puppies are born with parasites.

Ticks can cause serious problems to dogs where the latter have access to woods, fields, and vegetation in which large numbers of native mammals live. Ticks are usually found clinging to vegetation and attach themselves to animals passing by. They have eight legs and a heavy shield or shell-like covering on their upper surface. Only by keeping dogs away from tick-infested areas can ticks on dogs be prevented.

The flea is the single most common cause of skin and coat problems in dogs. There are 11,000 kinds of fleas which can transmit specific disorders like tapeworm and heartworm or transport smaller parasites onto your dog. The common tapeworm, for example, requires the flea as an intermediate host for completion of its life cycle.

A female flea can lay hundreds of eggs and these will become adults in less than three weeks. Depending on the temperature and the amount of moisture, large numbers of fleas can attack dogs. The ears of dogs, in particular, can play host to hundreds of fleas.

Fleas can lurk in crevices and cracks, carpets, and bedding for months, so frequent cleaning of your dog's environment is absolutely essential. If he is infected by other dogs, then have him bathed and "dipped," which means that he will be put into water containing a chemical that kills fleas. Your veterinarian will advise which dip to use, and your dog must be bathed for at least twenty minutes.

INTERNAL PARASITES

Four common internal parasites that may infect a dog are: roundworms, hookworms, whipworms, and tapeworms. The first three can be diagnosed by laboratory examination of the dog's stool, and tapeworms can be seen in the stool or attached to the hair around the anus. When a veterinarian determines what type of worm or worms are present, he then can advise the best treatment.

Roundworms, the dog's most common intestinal parasite, have a life cycle which permits complete eradication by worming twice, ten days apart. The first worming will remove all adults and the second will destroy all subsequently hatched eggs before they, in turn, can produce more parasites.

A dog in good physical condition is less susceptible to worm infestation than a weak dog. Proper sanitation and a nutritious diet help in preventing worms. One of the best preventive measures is to have clean, dry bedding for the dog, as this diminishes the possibility of reinfection due to flea or tick bites.

Heartworm infestation in dogs is passed by mosquitoes. Dogs with this disease tire easily, have difficulty in breathing, and lose weight despite a hearty appetite. Administration of preventive medicine throughout the spring, summer, and fall months is advised. A veterinarian must first take a blood sample from the dog to test for the presence of the disease, and if the dog is heartworm-free, pills or liquid medicine can be prescribed to protect against any infestation.

CANINE SENIOR CITIZENS

The processes of aging and gradual degenerative changes start far earlier in a dog than often observed, usually at about seven years of age. Your pet will become less active, will have a poorer appetite with increased thirst, there will be frequent periods of constipation and less than normal passage of urine. His skin and coat might become dull and dry and his hair will become thin and fall out. There is a tendency towards obesity in old age, which should be avoided by maintaining a regular exercise program. Remember, also, that your pet will be less able to cope with extreme heat, cold, fatigue, and change in routine.

There is the possibility of loss or impairment of hearing or eyesight. He may become bad-tempered more often than in the past. Visits to the vet should be more regular. Care of the teeth is also important in the aging dog. Indeed, the mouth can be a barometer of nutritional health. Degenerating gums, heavy tartar on the teeth, loose teeth, and sore lips are common. The worst of all diseases in old age, however, is neglect. Good care in early life will have its effect on your dog's later years; the nutrition and general health care of his first few years can determine his lifespan and the quality of his life. It is worth bearing in mind that the older, compared to the younger, animal needs more protein of good biological value, more vitamins A, B-complex, D and E, more calcium and iron, less fat and fewer carbohydrates.

The Dog Show World

Quality in the sense of "show quality" is determined by various factors such as the dog's health, physical condition, temperament, ability to move, and appearance. Breeders trying to breed show dogs are attempting to produce animals which come as close as possible to the word description of perfection as set out in the breed standard.

Keep in mind that dog show terminology varies from one place to another and even from one time to another. If you plan to show your dog, it always makes sense to check with your local or national breed club or with the national dog registry for the most complete, most up-to-date information regarding dog show regulations. In Great Britain, for example, match shows are known as limit shows. Age limit also differs, as dogs less than six months old may not be shown in Britain. Additionally, Britain has no point system for dogs, rather the dogs compete for championship certificates (C.C.s). Thus, point shows are known as championship shows in Great Britain.

MATCH SHOWS

One of the best ways to see if your puppy has championship potential is to attend a match show which is usually organized by the local kennel club or breed specialty club. Such shows provide a useful learning experience for the amateur and they offer you the opportunity to see how well your dog measures up to others being shown. There you can mingle with owners and professional handlers and pick up basic guidelines in showmanship, performance, and procedure. You can learn a great deal merely by closely observing the professional handlers performing in the ring.

The age limit is usually reduced to two months at match shows so that puppies can have four months of training before they compete in the regular shows when they reach six months. This time also helps them to overcome any "crowd nervousness." As class categories are the same as those included at a regular show, much experience can be gained in this informal atmosphere. Entry fees are low and paid at the door.

Before you go to a show, your dog should be trained to gait at a trot beside you, with head up and in a straight line. In the ring you will have to gait

Facing page: The most prestigious dog show in America is the Westminster Kennel Club Show held annually in Madison Square Garden, New York City.

around the edge with other dogs and then individually up and down the center runner. In addition, the dog must stand for examination by the judge, who will look at him closely and feel his head and body structure. He should be taught to stand squarely, hind feet slightly back and head up. He must hold the pose when you place his feet, and he must show a lively interest when you "bait" him, i.e., tempt him with a piece of boiled liver or a small squeak toy.

If your puppy receives praise and words of encouragement from the judges and other knowledgeable people, then you can begin to dream of Westminster or Crufts. It is always useful to visit such prestigious shows to see the best examples of all the various breeds.

After you have taken some handling lessons yourself, or employed a professional handler, the next step is participation in the point shows where you can earn points toward your dog's championship.

POINT SHOWS

Unlike match shows where your dog was judged on ring behavior, at point shows he will be judged on conformation to his breed standard. It is advisable to write to your national dog registry for information on how to register your dog and apply to dog shows. Below are the names and addresses of registries in the United States, Canada, Great Britain, and Australia.

The American Kennel Club
51 Madison Avenue
New York, NY 10010

The Canadian Kennel Club
111 Eglinton Avenue
East Toronto, Ontario M6S 4V7
Canada

The Kennel Club
1 Clarges Street Piccadilly,
London, W1Y 8AB, England

The Australian Kennel Club
Royal Show Grounds
Ascot Vale, Victoria, Australia.

Your local kennel club can provide you with the names and addresses of the show-giving superintendents (or show secretaries) near you, who will be staging the club's dog show for them, and where you must write for an official entry form. The forms will be mailed in a pamphlet called the "premium list" which will include the names of the judges for each breed, a list of the prizes and trophies, the names and addresses of the show-giving club, where the show will be held, as well as the rules and required procedure. Make certain that you fill in the form clearly and carefully and

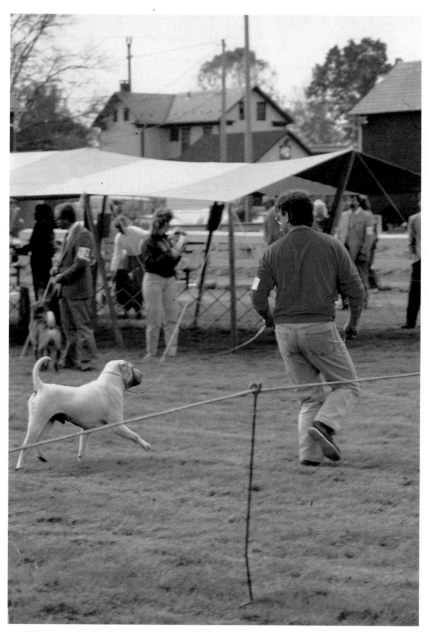

Enthusiasm for the breed at rare breed shows and mass media coverage led to the American Kennel Club's acceptance of the Shar-Pei in 1992. Today many Shar-Pei can be seen in the breed ring.

Four Paws offers an extensive line of grooming brushes, from slickers to curry brushes to pin brushes. These are sure to suit the grooming needs of every dog.

mail it in plenty of time.

Before then, however, you will have to decide in which classes your dog should compete. In the United States these are: Puppy, Novice, Bred-by-Exhibitor, American-bred and Open.

Puppy Classes are for dogs six months of age and over but under twelve months which are not champions. The age of a dog shall be calculated up to and inclusive of the first day of the show.

The *Novice Class* is for dogs six months of age and over, whelped in the United States or Canada, which have not, prior to the official closing date for entries, won three first prizes in the Novice Class, a first prize in Bred-by-Exhibitor, American-bred or Open Class or one or more points toward championship. In Britain, of course, dogs competing in the Novice Class must have been whelped in Britain.

The *Bred-by-Exhibitor Class*

is for dogs whelped in the U.S.A. or, if individually registered in the American Kennel Club Stud Book, for dogs in Canada that are six months of age and over. They must not be champions (although they may be in Britain), and must be owned wholly or in part by the person or the spouse of the person who was the breeder or one of the breeders of record. Dogs in this class must be handled by an owner or by a member of the immediate family of the owner. (This is not the case, however, in Britain.) Members of an immediate family for this purpose are: husband, wife, father, mother, son, daughter, brother and sister. This class has been referred to as the "breeder's showcase" as it is the one where the breeders can be justly proud of their achievements. The

American-bred Class is for all dogs (except champions) six months of age or over, whelped in the U.S.A. by reason of a mating that took place in the U.S.A.

The *Open Class* is for any dog six months of age or over, except in a member specialty club show held only for American-bred dogs, in which

The Shed 'N Blade is a tool used by groomers and handlers to eliminate dead, unwanted hair and allow for a healthy and vibrant coat.

Outdoor shows are popular throughout many regions of the country. Contact your local Shar-Pei club or the national kennel club for information about these events.

case the class is for American-bred dogs only.

In the United States and Canada, one does not enter the *Winners Class.* One earns the right to compete in it by winning first prize in one of the above classes. Winners Dog and Winners Bitch are the awards which carry points toward championship with them. Also

Specials Class for Best of Breed and for Best of Opposite Sex to Best of Breed. In Britain, the Reserve C.C. winners compete against each other for Best of Breed, not Best of Winners.

Best of Breed is the highest-placing dog in a given breed, and that winner then represents the particular breed in Group competition. Groups include: Sporting Dogs, Herding Dogs, Hounds, Working Dogs, Terriers, Toys, and Non-sporting Dogs. The judge of each Group selects first, second, third, and fourth

designated by the judge are the Reserve Winners Dog and the Reserve Winners Bitch (in Britain these are designated Reserve C.C. Dog and Reserve C.C. Bitch) but they do not receive any points. This award means simply that the dog or bitch receiving it are standing "in reserve" should the Winners Dog or Winners Bitch be disallowed through any technicality in the official show rules and regulations.

The dog and bitch then compete against each other for Best of Winners, and they also vie with the champions in the

place among the Best of Breed winners within specific Groups. First-place winners in each Group then compete for Best in Show.

A scale of points is printed in each dog-show catalog, and the number of points awarded in a breed depends on the number of dogs shown in competition. A win of three or more points at a show is called a "major." To attain championship, a dog must win a total of fifteen points under at least three different judges, and included in those fifteen points must be two majors (each under a different judge). A dog that accumulates fifteen points and no majors does not qualify for championship. A dog must win in keen competition. (This is the case in the United States but not in Great Britain. As there is no point system in Britain, it doesn't matter how many dogs are shown in competition. Championship Certificates are awarded at the discretion of the judge, however few dogs are competing.)

OBEDIENCE AND FIELD TRIALS

It should be mentioned that obedience trials, in which any purebred dog may compete, are often held in conjunction with conformation shows. Dogs are judged on performance rather than on how well they measure up to their breed standard. Many dogs that have already earned their championship in the conformation ring also compete for obedience trial degrees.

Two training accessories especially common with obedience trial enthusiasts are the hurdle (below) and the dumbbell (facing page). To see dogs performing with these and other field accessories, attend an obedience competition. Remember that training requires consistency and commitment, but the rewards are well worth the effort.

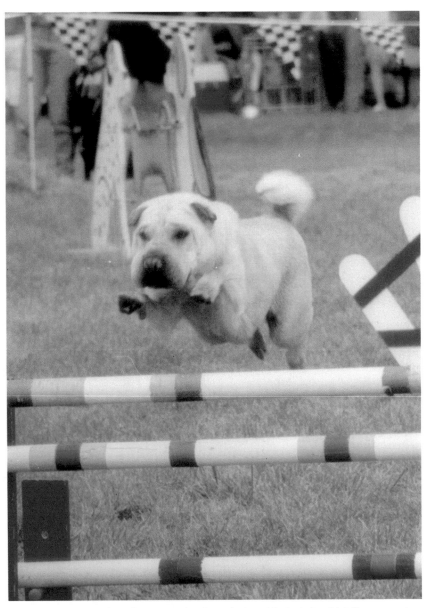

Agility trials are obstacle courses for dogs designed to test dogs' intelligence and coordination. They are just one more activity you and your Shar-Pei can enjoy doing together.

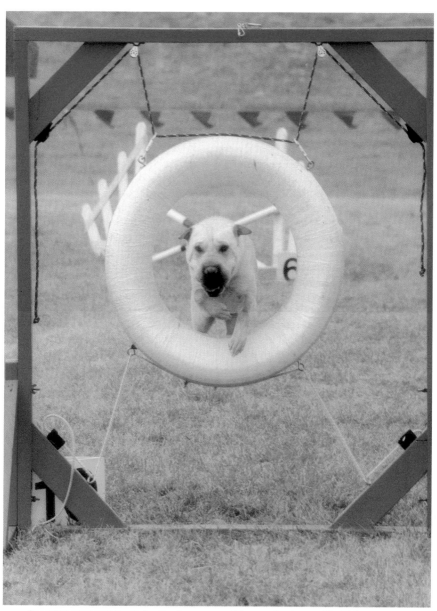

Shar-Pei coming through the tire jump, one of the events at an agility trial.

Some breeds, particularly hunting dogs and some of the hounds, also compete in field trials.

There are three classes in obedience: Novice, Open, and Utility. Tracking tests also are held. The respective degrees earned are: C.D., C.D.X., U.D., and T.D. These are: Companion Dog, Companion Dog Excellent, Utility Dog, and Tracking Dog. To earn a C.D., both the dog and his handler must perform six exercises together to the satisfaction of three different judges. Judges score the teams on a scale of zero to 200 points, and a score of 170 points or higher earns a dog a "leg" toward his obedience degree. A dog must achieve three "legs" for a C.D. Exercises in this Novice Class are: heel on lead and figure eight, stand for examination by a judge, heel off lead, long sit (sitting for a required number of minutes), long down (being down for several minutes), and recall (returning to his owner when called). After a dog gets his C.D., he then may try for his C.D.X. in Open obedience where he must jump over obstacles, retrieve items, and do more difficult exercises in three different trials. To achieve a U.D. title, a dog must do directed retrieving, jumping, and scent discrimination. To obtain a tracking degree, a dog competes in field trials where he "tracks" or follows a scent.

PRE-SHOW PREPARATIONS

As a very basic guide, the following list has been compiled to help you with your preparations for your first point show: the identification ticket sent by the show superintendent, a grooming table, a sturdy tack box in which to carry your dog's grooming tools, a leash to fasten him to the bench or stall and another show lead, your first aid kit, packaged "dog treats," and a supply of food and water for man and beast. Take the largest thermos you can find and a water dish. Remember to feed your dog after the show, not before, and make certain that he exercises and relieves himself before he enters the ring. Many experts think that an exercise pen is mandatory to eliminate the risk of exposing your dog to any diseases in the common exercise ground at shows, but before you bring one along, check the show rules to see if these are allowed. Moreover, exercise pens are useful as places where your dog can stretch out or rest during your travels or at a motel.

Even take time to think about what you are going to wear on the big day; sports clothes and

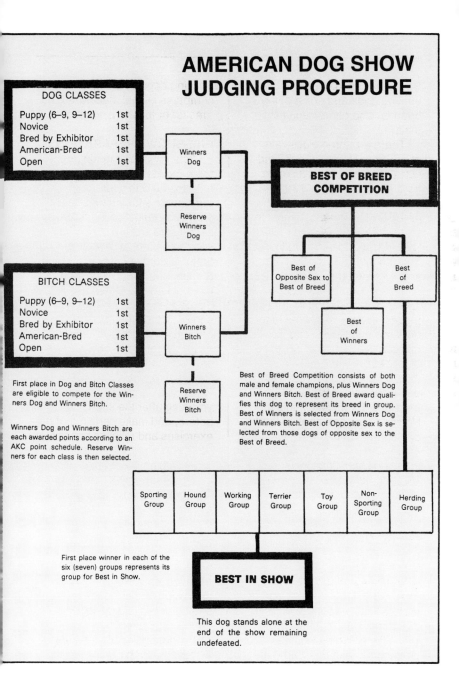

AMERICAN DOG SHOW JUDGING PROCEDURE

DOG CLASSES

Puppy (6–9, 9–12)	1st
Novice	1st
Bred by Exhibitor	1st
American-Bred	1st
Open	1st

Winners Dog

Reserve Winners Dog

BITCH CLASSES

Puppy (6–9, 9–12)	1st
Novice	1st
Bred by Exhibitor	1st
American-Bred	1st
Open	1st

Winners Bitch

Reserve Winners Bitch

BEST OF BREED COMPETITION

Best of Opposite Sex to Best of Breed

Best of Breed

Best of Winners

First place in Dog and Bitch Classes are eligible to compete for the Winners Dog and Winners Bitch.

Winners Dog and Winners Bitch are each awarded points according to an AKC point schedule. Reserve Winners for each class is then selected.

Best of Breed Competition consists of both male and female champions, plus Winners Dog and Winners Bitch. Best of Breed award qualifies this dog to represent its breed in group. Best of Winners is selected from Winners Dog and Winners Bitch. Best of Opposite Sex is selected from those dogs of opposite sex to the Best of Breed.

Sporting Group	Hound Group	Working Group	Terrier Group	Toy Group	Non-Sporting Group	Herding Group

First place winner in each of the six (seven) groups represents its group for Best in Show.

BEST IN SHOW

This dog stands alone at the end of the show remaining undefeated.

Shar-Pei clearing the bar jump at an agility trial.

low-heeled, comfortable shoes are the best. You certainly do not want to wear anything that would distract the judge's attention from your dog; you should merely provide an attractive background for him.

Although your knees may be trembling, try to appear self-confident as you gait (move) and set up the dog. The judging routine usually begins when the judge asks that the dogs be gaited in a circle around the ring while he observes their style, topline, head and tail carriage, reach and drive, and general balance. Avoid going too close to the dog in front of you. Make certain that the judge has an unrestricted view of your dog by keeping him on the inside of the circle, between you and the judge.

DOG SHOW ETIQUETTE

There are a few "golden rules" to be followed at dog shows which are worth mentioning at this stage. First of all, you are responsible for the behavior of your dog at all times. Keep your dog with you until the showing and keep him under control at all times. Constant vigilance is necessary as thefts have been known at dog shows, as well as poisoning and physical abuse of the animals by jealous exhibitors. You do not want your dog to become involved in a dog fight or taken for a walk by an irresponsible child or one too young to discipline him. In other words, you must not let your dog out of your sight.

Another golden rule is to be punctual; do not be late for your class. Remember that in the ring

Dog show exhibitors must be prepared to supervise and clean up after their dogs whenever on show grounds.

Squeaky toys and fuzzy animals are excellent tools to bait a dog in the show ring. Be sure not to distract your dog when the judge is examining him.

you must not communicate with the judge or fellow competitors. Watch the judge carefully and follow his instructions. Bear in mind that the ring is not the place to discipline or train your dog; it is too late at this stage! Whatever the judge's decision, accept it with good grace whether you win or lose. *Never* argue with a judge. Finally, remember to praise your dog for his efforts. It has been a long day for him as well.

"DOUBLE HANDLING"

Only one person should be handling your dog; there should not be other "handlers" in the audience who hope to influence his performance by the well-timed whistle, the "spontaneous" applause, or the secret signal. Such tactics are unsportsmanlike as they often distract the attention of other dogs. This so-called "double handling" is frowned upon by the American Kennel Club as a desperate measure resorted to by a desperate owner. Moreover, to try to prompt a win or stir up interest in your dog by bringing along your own cheering section is a futile gesture as a judge is concentrating on what he is doing and is not influenced by such subversive strategy. These people seem to be declaring that their dog cannot win by its own merits under normal conditions but needs some extra assistance.

Topographical Anatomy

SKULL

SMALL EARS

STOP

CREST

HIPPOPOTAMUS
MUZZLE

WITHERS

BACK

FLEW

WRINKLES

SHOULDER

BRISKET

ELBOW

FOREARM

WRIST

PASTERN

of the Shar-Pei

HIP

LOIN

HIGH SET TAIL

POINT OF RUMP

HORSE COAT

STIFLE OR KNEE

HOCK

Owner Concerns

By Chris Walkowicz

If something's worth doing at all, it's worth doing right. Behind the scenes of every gourmet feast, there's a lot of work, time and expense. Someone has to handle messy clean-up chores as well. The same is true of any worthwhile effort: a prize-winning novel, a community play, a good marriage, children, pets.

Conscientious owners know that there's more to raising a dog than picking one out, feeding it once a day and petting it if they feel the urge. Just as a fancy restaurant includes fine linens, flowers on the table and an attractive ambiance with the sustenance, being a top-quality dog owner means more than tossing a bone in the backyard now and then.

STRAYS

Although some people still have the mistaken idea that "a dog must be free," most are discovering that the world isn't what it once was. Loose dogs enjoying their "freedom" face all kinds of traumas: shotguns, poison, traps, oncoming trucks, dog pounds and the resulting euthanasia.

A dog without a home can rarely find a handout or even a rabbit to run down anymore. Garbage forays don't go far enough to fill an empty stomach, and they anger the person who is left to pick up the mess. Cars take their tolls on the highways. To combat these and other problems, good owners are taking steps to make sure their dogs remain welcome in society.

When a breeder is first contacted by a prospective buyer, the question is not simply, "Do you have a fenced yard?" but "Do you have a pen or a fenced yard—or do you plan to walk your dog on leash?" No option. If "none of the above" is the answer, it's bye-bye, buyer.

Children who are uncontrolled and unrestricted are obnoxious, cause damage and are a danger to themselves. Responsible people know that when they tell their children "No," it really is for their own good and that of others. It's not just a power ploy to deny them a privilege. Although it is difficult, there are reasons parents deny complete freedom to children, and there are reasons to deny it to dogs.

Dogs will be dogs. Loose animals are, at the least, a pain in the posterior and, at worst, a threat to themselves and others. Stray dogs bite, poop, scare kids, chase people, strew garbage, ruin lawns and gardens, kill other animals and produce unwanted litters.

OVERPOPULATION

The number of once-upon-a-time pets humanely euthanized annually in pounds and shelters is mind-boggling. These and the additional number of animals who die in agony—starvation, abuse, disease, trauma or road kills—were murdered by irresponsible owners and breeders as surely as if they aimed a gun and pulled the trigger. If animals were considered as living creatures instead of property by the court systems, many owners could be charged with negligence in their pets' deaths.

Neutering (spaying and castrating) means fewer animals, and fewer animals enable us to decrease the horrible statistics. Not only do we ascertain that none of our dog's pups become part of the canine carnage, but neutering also lowers the percentage of cancers and diseases of the reproductive system.

There are already plenty of dogs in the world without creating more. Anyone who wants one can find one immediately. It's only when people want specifics (i.e., a Pointer with great hunting ability; a Saint Bernard with lines that are hip-certified and show longevity; a Dachshund pup with the potential to go Best in Show) that someone needs to supply a demand.

It is true that a mixed-breed dog can make a great pet. Any dog, even one whose

background is unknown, might turn into your best pal. But you're taking your chances. There are already thousands of those to go around—no need to create more. Only someone who cares enough to obtain the knowledge to produce canines with specific physical characteristics, temperament and instincts has a right to add to the already-bulging and suffering canine population. Therefore, ethical breeders now sell companion pups with a spay/neuter clause, which requires the dog to be neutered at puberty or by the age of one year. Many also use the Limited Registration option with the American Kennel Club. This allows the dog itself to be registered and shown in obedience and instinct tests, but in case of a "mistake," none of its progeny can be registered.

Dog breeding, done properly, is an expensive proposition. It is also time-consuming, extra work, occasionally heartbreaking and often frustrating. Add all of these problems to the fact that a neutered pet is a healthier one, many pet—and even some show—owners now choose a sexless life for their dog.

LICENSING

Dog licenses are not another means to extract more money from your pocket for the local government, but rather they are

These beautiful black Shar-Pei are owned by Edward Bronson.

insurance for your dog. A dog license just might save your pet from euthanasia. Animal control officers compare the dog license to our own driver's licenses. It's an I.D. That tag hanging from his collar can be traced to the owner, which means a lost pet might be saved from the gas chamber. Licenses also contribute toward the care of the unwanted, forgotten and forlorn ex-pets who will pay the price for "freedom."

THEFT AND LOSS

It's terrifying when a dog owner first looks outdoors and sees the empty yard with the gate swinging open. When someone realizes his pet is gone, the heart takes a plummeting ride to the pit of the stomach.

Sometimes, no matter what precautions are taken, accidents happen—a child leaves a gate open or a well-behaved dog finds a rabbit on the other side of the fence too attractive to resist.

Owners should take action immediately to assure the pet's return. Don't wait a few hours to see if he'll come home. It may be too late.

To find a lost dog:

1. POSTERS—Have hundreds printed at a jiffy printer, preferably with a photo, and post every one. Someone who sees one poster may not retain the memory, but someone who sees 20 will remember. Describe the dog, always keeping in mind the fable of the blind men and the elephant. To a large man, a medium-sized dog may appear to be small; to a child, it may seem to be an elephant. In addition, a lost dog usually loses weight. It's better to print a lower estimate of his size and describe the breed, even if it's a well-known breed. Remember if the dog is gone for more than a few hours, a well-groomed animal can quickly become disheveled and appear unkempt.

2. SPREAD THE WORD—Tell the mail carrier (who's always on the alert for stray dogs). Call the neighbors and schools (kids enjoy helping and love dogs). Call the police, veterinarians, pounds, shelters and humane societies not only in your county but in the surrounding counties. Dogs travel many miles in search of the cat they spied . . . or home. Not all dogs have the homing instinct of Lassie. As soon as possible, visit animal organizations with your posters. Don't take their word that there is no such purebred on the premises. Most people wouldn't recognize one if it bit them—and then it would probably be too late.

3. ADVERTISE—Call the papers and the radio stations. Offer a reward (which should also be printed on the posters). Make it high enough to make it worthwhile for someone to return the dog, but low enough that it does not invite extortionists.

4. SEARCH—Never stop searching. Use an answering machine or have someone stay by the phone to answer any reports of the dog being sighted. Dogs have been found as long as six months after their loss.

5. HUMANE TRAP—Set a familiar object (a blanket or a crate with a favorite toy) on your porch or in your garage, along with bowls of food and water. If he does come home while you're out searching, he'll have a reason to stay.

6. PREVENTION—Fences, kennel runs and walking on leash. If the dog is a jumper or climber, make the fence higher or plant shrubs around to increase the distance and top the run. I.D. your dog with tags and a tattoo. Take photos, both *haute coiffure* and *au naturel.*

7. BE PREPARED—A lost dog is often terrified. Even those who are normally friendly can panic when called by a stranger, or even by someone they've known and loved all their lives. Use a lure: food, a kennelmate, an open car door, a bitch in season for a stud dog, a favorite toy or sound (like food pans, or a gunshot for a hunting dog).

Too often, also, dognappers are lured by a winsome face,

easy prey, or the potential easy money flashed by a purebred. The dognapper's booty is sometimes sold to people who are unaware of the circumstances. Most times, however, they're marketed to dog brokers, who fake papers and resell the dog. Worse yet, they might be sold to dog fighters (as bait or fighters) or laboratories (for experiments). Stolen dogs are difficult, if not impossible, to trace unless they can be positively identified.

TATTOO IDENTIFICATION

To prevent a much-loved family pet from ending his days in fear and agony, the best method of prevention is tattooing. Many dog clubs and veterinarians provide tattoo identification. By law, no laboratory may use a dog bearing a tattoo. Although some owners tattoo on the inside of the ear, most choose the inside of the rear thigh. An ear can be easily cut off.

Most American owners use their social security number, which is usually put on the inside of the dog's right hind thigh. Some use the dog's registration number, which goes on the inside of the left rear thigh. The area is first shaved and numbed. There is no pain, although a few dogs do not like the buzzing sound.

The characteristic wrinkles of the Shar-Pei are adorable and enticing; however, they do lend themselves to many skin problems and must be cleaned routinely.

Although this Shar-Pei pup is a cute little ball of wrinkles and rolls, he will grow into a large percentage of his coat and may even become a fairly tight-coated adult.

NO DOGS!

In Europe, dogs accompany their masters everywhere—to stores, buses and even in restaurants. Because the dogs are accustomed to public acceptance, they're well behaved and sit or lie quietly. Or is it because the pets are well behaved that they are accepted?

In the United States, however, "No Dogs"! signs are popping up like weeds—all over and too many. Because of bratty canines and careless owners, landlords demand a no-pets clause in leases. Parks restrict certain areas for pets if they're allowed at all. Many motels and hotels no longer admit anyone with a dog.

Many cities have a poop-scoop ordinance. Owners are required to clean up after their dogs or pay a fine. For too long, people have had the mistaken notion that their bad habits are not offensive to others, or even if they are, that's tough luck. These people claim, "It's our right to leave doggy doo-doo (drive carelessly, be sloppy drunk, blow smoke in your face or you fill in the blank). We aren't hurting anyone." Wrong. It's our right to own dogs but not to turn parks, sidewalks and public places into doggy latrines. Now we know our bad habits can be not only offensive but harmful to others, and we've got to straighten up and fly right, or we'll be flying solo.

If we want to continue this special bond between dogs and people, we must scoop poop, walk dogs on leash and train them to behave in public. It's no longer a good idea but a necessity that we attend classes and practice good manners. That demands confining pets and curtailing barking. It means no destruction of motel rooms, no jumping up when uninvited and no disgusting piles left behind—in other words, cleaning up our act.

RESCUE

Dog fanciers have recognized the need to spread good will beyond the home boundaries. There are too many strays, abuse cases and abandoned animals. Dogs in these situations need help, and they can't supply it themselves. Their so-called owners won't supply it.

Local and national clubs have organized rescue associations to aid in placing these needy dogs. Members volunteer to investigate situations, check out shelters and even to house a victim temporarily. Because of conditions where the animals may have suffered physically as well as mentally, many dogs need TLC and veterinary treatment before a new home is sought. Usually the dog is neutered before placement.

Occasionally, there is a waiting list for "orphans of the storm." Other times, a dog must be maintained and made well again before being adopted. All prospective homes are thoroughly screened so that the tragedy does not reoccur.

Medical care, boarding, adoption fees, transportation and routine expenses all mean that breed rescue programs need funds. Some samaritans foot the bills themselves. Clubs hold fundraising occasions which include bake sales, garage sales, recycling, tattoo clinics, auctions, matches, dog washes and dips and a rescue "check-off" included with the check for annual dues. Recipients of rescued dogs often respond and are, in some cases, required to make donations.

When these dogs are once again sound, they are placed in good homes. In this way, club members feel they are giving something back to the breed they love so much.

Breeders can assist in assuring that their pups won't someday be in need of rescue by including return clauses in their contracts. The breeder should always have first option to take the dog back if he needs to be placed. Follow up on pups with inquiries to see how they're doing, requests for photos to fill the breeder's scrapbook, and suggestions of training classes. Offering your assistance to groom or handle the dog and your availability to answer questions will help the new owner make it through tough times and offer assurance that one of your pups won't become a victim of our throw-away society.

PETS AND HEALTH: A FRIEND INDEED

By Diana Schellenberg
Excerpted from the December 1993 issue of the HARVARD HEALTH LETTER, ©1993, President and Fellows of Harvard College.

"I think I could turn and live with animals," Walt Whitman wrote, "they are so placid and self-contained." And as T. S. Eliot pointed out, animals are "such agreeable friends—they ask no questions, they pass no criticisms." Apparently the majority of Americans agree with the poets: 58% of households in the United States now include at least one pet. A 1992 survey sponsored by the American Veterinary Medical Association showed that cats, with a population of around 60 million, have surpassed dogs as America's favorite companion animal—a shift that probably comes as no surprise to cats, who have always acted as though they were number one. What with the cats and around

Make sure that children understand that their Shar-Pei pup is not a toy but a living thing that must be treated with love and respect.

52 million dogs, 12 million birds, and 5 million horses, Americans are sharing their daily lives with nearly 130 million of these creatures. In addition, around 8% of households keep fish and at least 4% have more unusual pets such as ferrets, gerbils, rabbits, or reptiles.

Most people who have companion animals consider them members of the family. Unlike humans in the household who have their ups and downs, most pets behave in fairly predictable ways and many offer unconditional affection. Dogs and cats typically spend most of their time in the house, and many sleep on their owners' beds. One measure of the value of their company is the billions of dollars that Americans spend each year on pet food, accessories, and veterinary care. And everyone has read about the elaborate markers that grieving pet owners erect to memorialize their departed companions.

Baby talk

People enjoy their animals, and being with them stirs a sense of security and of being needed. Pets, regardless of their age, fill the role of an infant or young child in the household, according to researcher Alan Beck, who heads the Center for Applied Ethology and Human-Animal Interaction at the Purdue University School of Veterinary Medicine. He and psychiatrist Aaron Katcher did pioneering studies of the connection between humans and animals during the 1970s and 1980s, when both were at the University of Pennsylvania.

Drs. Beck and Katcher found that people talk to their pets as if they were young infants. They move close to the animal's head, use a higher-pitched voice, and speak more softly and slowly than usual. They insert pauses as if the animal were answering back. Their facial expressions also soften, which may be one reason why people are perceived as more attractive and more approachable when they are with a pet.

Warm fuzzies

Only during the past few decades have scientists become interested in the beneficial effects that pets may have on human health. One way to assess the effect is to measure the short-term physiological impact of contact with an animal. So far, experiments using children and college students have found that watching or petting and talking with an animal can lower blood pressure and heart rate.

Short-term studies have also demonstrated that interacting with animals can reduce mental distress. For college students in a laboratory setting, petting a friendly dog lowered not only their blood pressure and heart rate but also their anxiety level, as measured by a standard test. Researchers found that patients who watched fish in an aquarium while they waited to have oral surgery did just as well as those who underwent hypnosis to reduce anxiety and discomfort during the surgery. These results help explain why aquariums are so popular in dental and medical waiting rooms.

Most epidemiologic studies comparing people with and without pets have suggested that those who share their lives with animals have higher morale and lower rates of depression. Such studies do not tell us, however, whether pet owning leads to better psychological health or whether it's healthier people who acquire pets in the first place.

Heartfelt support

A large Australian study reported in 1992 did not answer this question but did indicate that pet owners have fewer risk factors for heart disease than people without such companions. The researchers assessed common predictors of cardiovascular problems in 5,741 people who attended a free screening clinic in Melbourne. Overall, the 13.6% who owned pets had lower systolic blood pressure and lower total cholesterol and triglyceride levels than non-owners. These differences were significant despite variations in participants' smoking habits, diet, body height and weight, and socioeconomic status. It did not appear to matter if pets had four legs, wings, or scales: all pet owners benefited whether or not they had pets that needed regular exercise.

Although the association between pet ownership and an apparent reduction in cardiovascular risk is an interesting finding, it does not demonstrate that pets can guard their masters against heart disease or any other illness. This kind of evidence can be gained only from *prospective* studies, where researchers, in anticipation of possible patterns or correlations, design research to analyze ongoing events. In this instance, researchers would need to track the health status of many pet owners and non-owners over a long period of time.

So far, the largest prospective investigation of the effect of pet owning was done by epidemiologist Judith Siegel of the University of California, Los Angeles. For one year Dr. Siegel monitored stressful life

The Shar-Pei, one of the earliest breeds of dog, came close to extinction during the 1960s. Owner, Theresa Stewart events, use of physician services, and the psychological well-being of 938 people who were covered by Medicare and enrolled in a health maintenance organization. The 37% of participants who owned pets made fewer visits to the doctor than people without animal companions. This was true regardless of the chronic health problems they had at the beginning of the study period, or of their sex, age, race, education, income, employment status, and degree of social support from other people.

When family members or friends became severely ill or died, pets seemed to be a "stress buffer" for their bereaved human companions. People without pets made more physician visits as stressful events accumulated in their lives, but pet owners—especially those with dogs—did not follow this pattern. Reporting her findings in the *Journal of Personality and Social Psychology,* Dr. Siegel speculated that elderly people sometimes go to the doctor because they need companionship, or because loneliness exacerbates their health concerns.

Pets, particularly dogs, appear at least partially to satisfy the need for company. About 25% of people in Dr. Siegel's study said that their pets made them feel secure, and 21% said they felt loved by their animals. These findings, coupled with results from smaller inquiries, suggest that the social and psychological support that people gain from pets may reduce their need for the attention of health care providers.

Animal companionship may also be a boon to people recovering from an acute illness. A prospective study of 92 people admitted to a coronary care unit for confirmed or suspected myocardial infarction found that those with animals were more likely to be alive one year later than those without pets.

The dark underbelly

The benefits of pet owning seem so obvious—especially after a brisk walk with a lively dog or an evening curled up with a purring puss—that it is tempting to brush aside the negative aspects of living with animals. Unfortunately, problems can arise from allergies, bites, or infections.

Roughly 1.5% of the general population and 25% of patients being treated for allergies are sensitive to dogs or cats. When doctors recommend that the offending animal be removed from the home, pet-owning patients often resist. Recent research suggests that people who are allergic to cats may be able to coexist with them if they wash the cat once a week, accustom the animal to spending more time outdoors, eliminate carpeting, use air filters, and follow a rigorous housecleaning schedule. (Researchers, however, do not report what sort of protective gear pet owners should don for the weekly bath.)

Animal bites pose an even more obvious health problem. Bites account for 1% of all visits to hospital emergency rooms, although about 80% of these injuries are minor. Many bites need not have occurred in the first place. Children should be taught how to approach and handle pets, read their warning signals, and avoid high-risk situations. Dog owners must do their part by training their dogs and by keeping potentially dangerous animals leashed or fenced.

Infectious diseases can be spread when a bite deposits organisms from the animal's mouth into a wound. These infections range from the annoying to the potentially deadly, such as rabies. Any bite that breaks the skin calls for prompt medical attention. Fortunately, taking a few simple measures can reduce the risk.

The difficulty of balancing the benefits and risks of sharing one's life with an animal may be illustrated most poignantly by the pet owner with AIDS, who needs a loving companion but whose impaired immune system is particularly vulnerable to certain infections. Volunteer organizations help AIDS patients keep their pets by offering food deliveries, in-home pet care, foster care, and adoption services when the need arises.

Prescription pets

In the therapeutic arena, there is a growing appreciation for the roles that companion animals can play in institutions and in the world at large. Dogs have long been used as a source of support for troubled children and for psychiatric patients, and today many volunteers take their pets to visit local nursing homes. Assistance dogs serve as surrogate eyes, ears, or legs for thousands of people with disabilities.

For most people pets are neither a panacea nor a plague. Responsible pet ownership entails a commitment to the animal and a promise to train it properly and to provide it with adequate care. The return on this investment can be considerable: a loving companion, an antidote to stress, and perhaps a reason for regular exercise, all wrapped up in fur or feathers.

Breeding

As the owner of a purebred dog, you may have considered breeding your pet at one time or another. If your dog is a beloved family pet, and not a show dog, you should *not* breed your dog. Breeding is not a hobby for pet owners, but rather a demanding, complicated vocation that is not to be dabbled with. Many people have thought of breeding as an easy-money opportunity: buy two dogs and let them do the work. The rule of thumb is: if you're making money by breeding dogs, you're doing something wrong!

Consider the time and money involved just to get your bitch into breeding condition and then to sustain her throughout pregnancy and afterwards while she tends her young. You will be obligated to house, feed, groom, and housebreak the puppies until good homes can be found for them; and, lest we forget, there will be periodic trips to the vet for check-ups, wormings, and inoculations. Common sense should tell you that it is indeed cruel to bring unwanted or unplanned puppies into an already crowded canine world; only negligent pet owners allow this to happen. Recognizing the number of dogs, purebred and mixed breeds, pet-, show- and breeding-quality, that are put to sleep annually, responsible breeders require that all pet animals be neutered. This

condition most often is incorporated into the selling contract. The motives of good breeders are clear: avoid the manufacturing and mass-producing of average and below-average dogs; control the overblown canine population; concentrate on the improvement of purebred bloodlines. Breeding is a noble calling and unless you can improve the breed, you should not consider breeding your animal. Despite all of the obvious virtues of breeding texts, no book could ever prepare a person for breeding. What a heart-breaking and tragic experience to lose an entire litter because a good-intentioned pet owner wasn't aware of potential genetic complications, didn't recognize a breech birth, or couldn't identify the signals of a struggling bitch! Possibly the dam could be lost as well!

Before you take any step towards mating your bitch, think carefully about why you want her to give birth to a litter of puppies. If you feel she will be deprived in some way if she is not bred, if you think your children will learn from the experience, if you have the mistaken notion that you will make money from this great undertaking, think again. A dog can lead a perfectly happy, healthy, normal life without having been mated; in fact, spaying a female and neuterin a male helps them become better, longer-lived pets, as they are not so anxious to search for a mate in an effort to relieve their sexual tensions and have a diminished risk of cancer. As for giving the children a lesson in sex education, this is hardly a valid reason for breeding your dog. And on an economic level, it takes not only years of hard work (researching pedigrees and bloodlines, studying genetics, among other things), but it takes plenty of capital (money, equipment, facilities) to make a decent profit from dog breeding. Why most dedicated breeders are lucky just to break even. If you have only a casual interest in dog breeding, it is best to leave this pastime to those who are more experienced in such matters, those who consider it a serious hobby and a real vocation. If you have bought a breeder– or show-quality canine, one that may be capable of producing champions, and if you are just starting out with this

Breeding dogs requires more than book knowledge. In dogs, breech presentation is not uncommon and the breeder must be prepared to handle this situation and guide the puppy so that neither the pup nor the bitch is injured.

breeding venture, seek advice from the seller of your dog, from other veteran breeders, and from your veterinarian before you begin.

The following sections on reproduction are intended for academic value only. This is not a "How-to" chapter on breeding, nor a step-by-step approach for the novice for getting started. Hopefully the reader will understand the depth and complexity of breeding as well as the expected ethical and moral obligations of persons who

choose to do so—and never attempt it.

THE FEMALE "IN SEASON"

A bitch may come into season (also known as "heat" or estrus) once or several times a year, depending on the particular breed and the individual dog. Her first seasonal period, that is to say, the time when she is capable of being fertilized by a male dog, may occur as early as six months with some breeds. If you own a female and your intention is *not* to breed her, by

Ideally the puppy will be delivered in the normal head-first position.

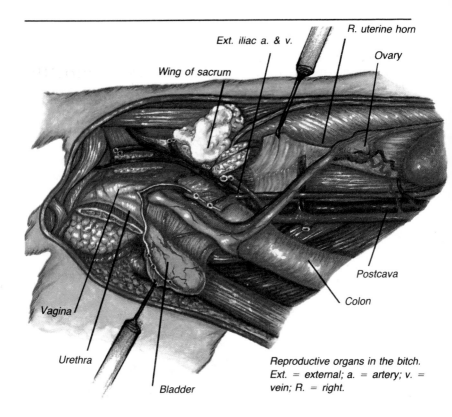

Reproductive organs in the bitch. Ext. = external; a. = artery; v. = vein; R. = right.

The reproductive system of the female dog consists of a highly specialized system of organs situated to the rear of the animal.

all means discuss with the vet the possibility of having her spayed: this means before she reaches sexual maturity.

The first sign of the female's being in season is a thin red discharge, which may increase for about a week; it then changes color to a thin yellowish stain, which lasts about another week. Simultaneously, there is a swelling of the vulva, the exterior portion of the female's reproductive tract; the soft, flabby vulva indicates her readiness to mate. Around this second week or so ovulation occurs, and this is the crucial period for her to be bred, if this is what you have in mind for her. It is during this middle phase of the heat cycle when conception can take place. Just remember that there is great variation from bitch to bitch with regard to how often they come into heat, how long the heat cycles last, how long the period of ovulation lasts, and how much time elapses between heat cycles. Generally, after the third week of heat, the vulval swelling decreases and the estrus period ceases for several months.

It should be mentioned that the female will probably lose her puppy coat, or at least shed part of it, about three months after she has come into season. This is the time when her puppies would have been weaned, had she been mated, and females generally drop coat at this time.

With female dogs, there are few, if any, behavioral changes during estrus. A bitch may dart out of an open door to greet all available male dogs that show an interest in her, and she may occasionally raise her tail and

Each egg within the female is surrounded by a wall that normally takes many sperm to penetrate. In this way, it is more likely that only the strongest sperm will fertilize the egg. A fertile female in season usually has a number of eggs, known as gametes.

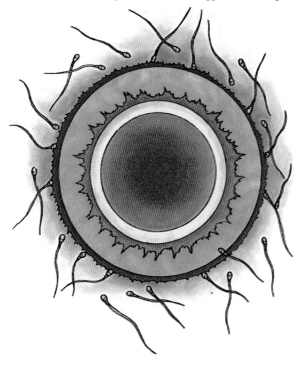

assume a mating stance, particularly if you pet her lower back; but these signs are not as dramatic as those of the sexually mature male. He himself does not experience heat cycles; rather, he is attracted to the female during all phases of her seasonal period. He usually becomes more aggressive and tends to fight with other males, especially over females in heat. He tends to mark his territory with urine to attract females and at the same time to warn other competitive males. It is not uncommon to see him mount various objects, and people, in an effort to satisfy his mature sexual urges.

If you are a homeowner and you have an absolutely climb-proof and dig-proof run within your yard, it may be safe to leave your bitch in season there. But then again it may not be a wise idea, as there have been cases of males mating with females right through chain-link fencing! Just to be on the safe side, shut her indoors during her heat periods and don't let her outdoors until you are certain the estrus period is over. Never leave a bitch in heat outdoors, unsupervised, even for a minute so that she can defecate or urinate. If you want to prevent the neighborhood dogs from hanging around your doorstep, as they inevitably will do when

they discover your female is in season, take her some distance away from the house before you let her do her business. Otherwise, these canine suitors will be attracted to her by the arousing odor of her urine, and they will know instinctively that she isn't far from her scented "calling card." If you need to walk your bitch, take her in the car to a nearby park or field for a chance to stretch her legs. Remember that after about three weeks, and this varies from dog to dog, you can let her outdoors again with no worry that she can have puppies until the next heat period.

If you are seriously considering breeding your dog, first talk to as many experienced breeders as possible and read up on the subject in specific books and articles. Only when you are fully aware of the demands and responsibilities of breeding should you make your final decision. It must be stated here that there is no shortage of fine dogs in need of good homes, nor is there likely to be in the foreseeable future. So, if

Facing page: The male reproductive system includes the penis and testicles. When not excited, the penis is withdrawn into the dog's body.

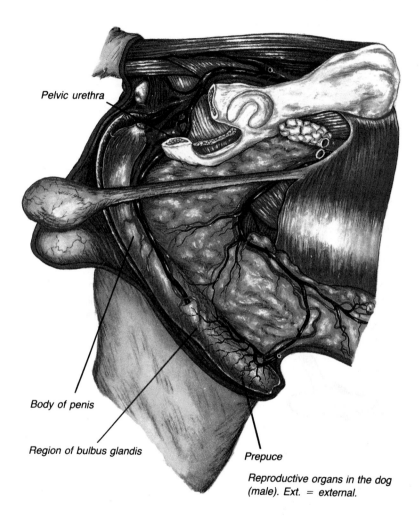

Pelvic urethra

Body of penis

Region of bulbus glandis

Prepuce

Reproductive organs in the dog (male). Ext. = external.

PERPETUAL WHELPING CHART

Bred / Due	Days
Bred—Jan.	1 2 3 4 5 6 7 8 9 10 11 12 13 14 15 16 17 18 19 20 21 22 23 24 25 26 27 28 29 30 31
Due—March	5 6 7 8 9 10 11 12 13 14 15 16 17 18 19 20 21 22 23 24 25 26 27 28 29 30 31 — *April* 1 2 3 4
Bred—Feb.	1 2 3 4 5 6 7 8 9 10 11 12 13 14 15 16 17 18 19 20 21 22 23 24 25 26 27 28
Due—April	5 6 7 8 9 10 11 12 13 14 15 16 17 18 19 20 21 22 23 24 25 26 27 28 29 30 — *May* 1 2
Bred—Mar.	1 2 3 4 5 6 7 8 9 10 11 12 13 14 15 16 17 18 19 20 21 22 23 24 25 26 27 28 29 30 31
Due—May	3 4 5 6 7 8 9 10 11 12 13 14 15 16 17 18 19 20 21 22 23 24 25 26 27 28 29 30 31 — *June* 1 2
Bred—Apr.	1 2 3 4 5 6 7 8 9 10 11 12 13 14 15 16 17 18 19 20 21 22 23 24 25 26 27 28 29 30
Due—June	3 4 5 6 7 8 9 10 11 12 13 14 15 16 17 18 19 20 21 22 23 24 25 26 27 28 29 30 — *July* 1 2
Bred—May	1 2 3 4 5 6 7 8 9 10 11 12 13 14 15 16 17 18 19 20 21 22 23 24 25 26 27 28 29 30 31
Due—July	3 4 5 6 7 8 9 10 11 12 13 14 15 16 17 18 19 20 21 22 23 24 25 26 27 28 29 30 31 — *August* 1 2
Bred—June	1 2 3 4 5 6 7 8 9 10 11 12 13 14 15 16 17 18 19 20 21 22 23 24 25 26 27 28 29 30
Due—August	3 4 5 6 7 8 9 10 11 12 13 14 15 16 17 18 19 20 21 22 23 24 25 26 27 28 29 30 31 — *Sept.* 1
Bred—July	1 2 3 4 5 6 7 8 9 10 11 12 13 14 15 16 17 18 19 20 21 22 23 24 25 26 27 28 29 30 31
Due—September	2 3 4 5 6 7 8 9 10 11 12 13 14 15 16 17 18 19 20 21 22 23 24 25 26 27 28 29 30 — *Oct.* 1 2
Bred—Aug.	1 2 3 4 5 6 7 8 9 10 11 12 13 14 15 16 17 18 19 20 21 22 23 24 25 26 27 28 29 30 31
Due—October	3 4 5 6 7 8 9 10 11 12 13 14 15 16 17 18 19 20 21 22 23 24 25 26 27 28 29 30 31 — *Nov.* 1 2
Bred—Sept.	1 2 3 4 5 6 7 8 9 10 11 12 13 14 15 16 17 18 19 20 21 22 23 24 25 26 27 28 29 30
Due—November	3 4 5 6 7 8 9 10 11 12 13 14 15 16 17 18 19 20 21 22 23 24 25 26 27 28 29 30 — *Dec.* 1 2
Bred—Oct.	1 2 3 4 5 6 7 8 9 10 11 12 13 14 15 16 17 18 19 20 21 22 23 24 25 26 27 28 29 30 31
Due—December	3 4 5 6 7 8 9 10 11 12 13 14 15 16 17 18 19 20 21 22 23 24 25 26 27 28 29 30 31 — *Jan.* 1 2
Bred—Nov.	1 2 3 4 5 6 7 8 9 10 11 12 13 14 15 16 17 18 19 20 21 22 23 24 25 26 27 28 29 30
Due—January	3 4 5 6 7 8 9 10 11 12 13 14 15 16 17 18 19 20 21 22 23 24 25 26 27 28 29 30 31 — *Feb.* 1
Bred—Dec.	1 2 3 4 5 6 7 8 9 10 11 12 13 14 15 16 17 18 19 20 21 22 23 24 25 26 27 28 29 30 31
Due—February	2 3 4 5 6 7 8 9 10 11 12 13 14 15 16 17 18 19 20 21 22 23 24 25 26 27 28 — *March* 1 2 3 4

your object in breeding is merely to produce more dogs, you are strongly encouraged to reconsider your objective.

WHEN TO BREED

It is usually best to breed a bitch when she comes into her second or third season. Plan in advance the time of year which is best for you, taking into account your own schedule of activities (vacations, business trips, social engagements, and so on). Make sure you will be able to set aside plenty of time to assist with whelping of the newborn pups and caring for the dam and her litter for the next few weeks. At the very least, it probably will take an hour or so each day just to feed and clean up after the brood—but undoubtedly you will find it takes

much longer if you stop to admire and play with the youngsters periodically! Refrain from selling the litter until it is at least six weeks old, keeping in mind that a litter of pups takes up a fair amount of space by then. It will be your responsibility to provide for them until they have been weaned from their mother, properly socialized, housebroken, and ready to go to new homes (unless you plan to keep them all). Hopefully, as strongly recommended, you will have already lined up buyers for the pups in advance of their arrival into this world.

CHOOSING THE STUD

You can plan to breed your female about six-and-one-half months after the start of her last season, although a variation of a

Whelping box prepared with "pig rails," bars on either side of the box to prevent the bitch from rolling on the puppies.

month or two either way is not unusual. Do some research into the various bloodlines within your breed and then choose a stud dog and make arrangements well in advance. If you are breeding for show stock, which will command higher prices than pet-quality animals, a mate should be chosen very carefully. He should complement any deficiencies (bad traits) that your female may have, and he should have a good show record or be the sire of show winners, if he is old enough to have proven himself. If possible, the bitch and stud should have several ancestors in common within the last two or three generations, as such combinations have been known, generally, to "click" best.

The owner of a stud dog usually charges a stud fee for use of the animal's services. This does not always guarantee a litter, but if she fails to conceive, chances are you may be able to breed your female to that stud again. In some instances the owner of the stud will agree to take a "first pick of the litter" in place of a fee. You should, of course, settle all details beforehand, including the possibility of a single puppy surviving, deciding the age at which the pup is to be taken, and so forth.

If you plan to raise a litter that will be sold exclusively as pets, and if you merely plan to make use of an available male (not a top stud dog), the most important selection point involves temperament. Make sure the dog is friendly, as well as healthy, because a bad disposition can be passed on to his puppies—and this is the worst of all traits in a dog destined to be a pet. If you are breeding pet-quality dogs, a "stud fee

Each puppy is delivered in a separate membranous sac. This sac must be removed by the bitch without delay—if not, the breeder must come immediately to the assistance of the pup.

puppy," not necessarily the choice of the litter, is the usual payment. Don't breed indiscriminately; be sure you will be able to find good homes for each of the pups, or be sure you have the facilities to keep them yourself, *before* you plan to mate your dog.

PREPARATION FOR BREEDING

Before you breed your female, make sure she is in good health. She should be neither too thin nor too fat. Any skin disease *must* be cured first so that it is not passed on to the puppies. If she has worms, she should be wormed before being bred or within three weeks after the mating. It is generally considered a good idea to revaccinate her against distemper and hepatitis before the puppies are born.

The female will probably be ready to breed twelve days after the first colored discharge appears. You can usually make arrangements to board her with the owner of the stud for a few days, to insure her being there at the proper time; or you can take her to be mated and bring her home the same day if you live near enough to the stud's owner. If the bitch still appears receptive she may be bred again two days later, just to make certain the mating was successful. However, some females never

Newborn pups are very susceptible to chills, so the breeder must dry the puppy off thoroughly and place it in a temperature-controlled puppy box.

show signs of willingness, so it helps to have an experienced breeder on hand. In fact, you both may have to assist with the mating by holding the animals against each other to ensure the "tie" is not broken, that is, to make certain copulation takes place.

Usually the second day after the discharge changes color is the proper time to mate the bitch, and she may be bred for about three days following this time. For an additional week or so, she may have some discharge and attract other dogs by her odor; but she should not be bred.

Once she has been bred, keep her far from all other male dogs, as they have the capacity to impregnate her again and sire some of her puppies. This could prove disastrous where purebred puppies.

THE FEMALE IN WHELP

You can expect the puppies nine weeks from the day of the mating, although 61 days is as common as 63. Gestation, that period when the pups are developing inside their mother, varies among individual bitches. During this time the female should receive normal care and exercise. If she was overweight at the start, don't increase her food right away; excess weight at whelping time can be a problem with some dogs. If she is on the thin side, however, supplement her meal or meals with a portion of milk and biscuit at noontime. This will help build her up and put weight on her.

You may want to add a mineral and vitamin supplement to her diet, on the advice of your veterinarian, since she will need an extra supply not only for herself but for the puppies growing inside her. As the mother's appetite increases, feed her more. During the last two weeks of pregnancy, the pups grow enormously and the mother will have little room for food and less of an appetite. She should be tempted with meat, liver, and milk, however.

As the female in whelp grows heavier, cut out violent exercise and jumping from her usual routine. Although a dog used to such activities will often play with the children or run around voluntarily,

"Pooping" the puppies, or rubbing the bowels and genitals to stimulate elimination, may be necessary if the bitch doesn't tend to this herself.

restrain her for her own sake.

A sign that whelping is imminent is the loss of hair around her breasts. This is nature's way of "clearing a path" so that the puppies will be able to find their source of nourishment. As parturition draws near, the breasts will have swelled with milk and the nipples will have enlarged and darkened to a rosy pink. If the hair in the breast region does not shed for some reason, you can easily cut it short with a pair of scissors or comb it out so that it does not mat and become a hindrance to the suckling pups later on.

The breeder must actively partake in cleaning the pup after feedings. Hands-on contact serves as the initial step in socialization— accustoming the pup to his human family.

PREPARING FOR THE PUPPIES

Prepare a whelping box a few days before the puppies are due, and allow the mother to sleep there overnight or to spend some time in it during the day to become accustomed to it. This way she is less likely to try to have her pups under the front porch or in the middle of your bed. A variety of places will serve, such as the corner of your cellar or garage (provided these places are warm and dry). An unused room, such as a dimly lit spare bedroom, can also serve as the place for delivery. If the weather is warm, a large outdoor dog house will do, as long as it is well protected from rain, drafts, and the cold—and enclosed by fencing or a run. A whelping box serves to separate mother and puppies from visitors and other distractions. The walls should be high enough to restrain the puppies yet low enough to allow the mother to take a short respite from her brood after she has fed them. Four feet square is minimum size (for most dogs) and six-to-eight-inch high walls will keep the pups in until they begin to climb; then side walls should be built up so that the young ones cannot wander away from their nest. As the puppies grow, they really need more

over the whole area will make excellent bedding and be absorbent enough to keep the surface warm and dry. These should be removed daily and replaced with another thick layer. An old quilt or washable blanket makes better footing for the nursing puppies than slippery newspaper during the first week; this is also softer for the mother to lie on.

Be prepared for the actual

Bottle-feeding may be necessary with particularly large litters or with a bitch who has become overly stressed or neglectful or whose milk has gone bad.

room anyway, so double the space with a very low partition down the middle of the box, and soon you will find them naturally housebreaking themselves. Puppies rarely relieve themselves where they sleep. Layers of newspapers spread

whelping several days in advance. Usually the mother will tear up papers, refuse food, and become restless. These may be false alarms; the real test is her temperature, which will drop to below 100°F (38°C) about twelve hours before whelping. Take her temperature with a rectal thermometer, morning and evening, and usher her to her whelping box when her temperature goes down. Keep a close watch on her and make sure she stays safely indoors (or outdoors in a safe enclosure); if she is let outside, unleashed, or allowed to roam freely, she could wander off and start to go into labor. It is possible that she could whelp anywhere, and this could be unfortunate if she needs your assistance.

WHELPING

Usually little help is needed from you, but it is wise to stay close to be sure that the mother's lack of experience (if this is her first time) does not cause an unnecessary complication. Be ready to help when the first puppy arrives, for it could smother if she does not break the amniotic membrane enclosing it. She should tear open the sac and start licking the puppy, drying and stimulating it. Check to see that all fluids have

Using simple genetic rules, an owner can predict to some degree the traits that the offspring of a given mating can exhibit. The six possible ways in which a pair of determiners can unite are illustrated on this Mendelian expectation chart. Ratios apply to expectancy over large numbers, except in lines 1, 2, and 6 where exact expectancy is realized in every litter.

MENDELIAN EXPECTATION CHART

been cleared from the pup's nostrils and mouth after the mother has licked her youngster clean; otherwise the pup may have difficulty breathing. If the mother fails to tear open the sac and stimulate the newborn's breathing, you can do this yourself by tearing the sack with your hands and then gently rubbing the infant with a soft, rough towel. The afterbirth attached to the puppy by the long umbilical cord, should follow the birth of each puppy. Watch to be sure that each afterbirth is expelled, for the retention of this material can cause infection. In her instinct for cleanliness the mother will probably eat the afterbirth after severing the umbilical cord. One or two meals of this will not hurt her; they stimulate her milk supply, as well as labor, for remaining pups. However, eating too many afterbirths can make her lose appetite for the food she needs to feed her pups and regain her strength. So remove the rest of

Prior to birth, the developing pups are housed in the horns of the uterus.

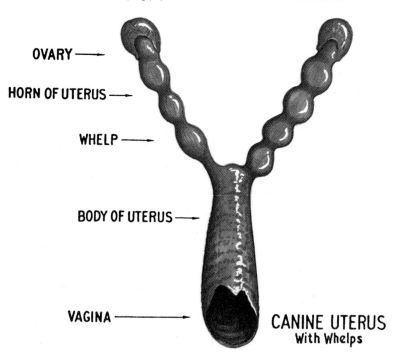

OVARY ——→

HORN OF UTERUS ——→

WHELP ——→

BODY OF UTERUS ——→

VAGINA ——————→

CANINE UTERUS
With Whelps

OVARY

HORN OF UTERUS

BLADDER —

BODY OF UTERUS

CANINE UTERUS
Before mating

VAGINA

The canine uterus is quite different from the human uterus. Besides the difference in shape, the canine uterus is designed to house an average of five to eight offspring.

them, along with the wet newspapers, and keep the box dry and clean.

If the mother does not bite the cord or bites it too close to the puppy's body, take over the job to prevent an umbilical hernia. Tearing is recommended, but you can cut the cord, about two inches from the body, with a sawing motion with scissors that have been sterilized in alcohol. Then dip the end of the cut cord in a shallow dish of iodine; the cord will dry up and fall off in a few days.

The puppies should follow each other at intervals of not more than half an hour. If more time goes past and you are sure there are still pups to come, taking the mother for a brisk walk outside may start labor again. If she is actively straining without producing a puppy, the youngster may be presented backward, a so-called "breech" birth. Careful assistance with a well-lubricated finger to feel for the puppy or to ease it back may help, but never attempt to pull it out by force. This could cause serious damage, so seek the services of an expert—your veterinarian or an experienced breeder.

Even the best planned breeding can bear unexpected problems and complications. Therefore, do not rely solely on textbook knowledge of breeding and genetics. Experienced breeders and veterinarians will generally lend their words of wisdom—take full advantage of their generosity. Mere trial and error is no basis for any responsible breeding program.

If *anything* seems wrong during labor or parturition, waste no time in calling your veterinarian, who will examine the bitch and, if necessary, give her hormones to stimulate the birth of the remaining puppies.

You may want his experience in whelping the litter even if all goes well. He will probably prefer to have the puppies born at his hospital rather than getting up in the middle of the night to come to your home. The mother would, no doubt, prefer to stay at home; but you can be sure she will get the best of care in a veterinary hospital. If the puppies are born at home, and all goes as it should, watch the mother carefully afterward. Within a day or two of the birth, it is wise to have the veterinarian check her and the pups to ensure that all is well.

Be sure each puppy finds a teat and starts nursing right away, as these first few meals supply colostral antibodies to help him fight disease. As soon

Cells reproduce by a process called mitosis, in which the cells divide, forming two identical cells.

PUPPY GROWTH AND BREEDER RESPONSIBILITY	
AGE	**REQUIRED CARE/EXPECTED DEVELOPMENT**
WEEKS 1–2	Helpless; dam must provide constant care; owner must ensure warmth and cleanliness; puppy nurses, crawls, needs stimulation for elimination; sleeps 90% of time.
WEEKS 3–4	Owner sustains optimum environment; puppy is alert, laps from bowl, takes first steps; defecates on its own; baby teeth emerge; barks, wags tail.
WEEKS 4–5	Ambles, growls, and bites; play and interaction increase; human contact limited but essential; learning begins.
WEEKS 5–6	Weaning; human socialization vital; pack order apparent; sex play; explores and sleeps less.
WEEKS 6–8	Two to three daily meals; puppy accustomed to human family; breeder initiates housetraining; first veterinary visit; wary of the unknown.

as he is dry, hold each puppy to a nipple for a good meal without competition. Then he may join his littermates in the whelping box, out of his mother's way while she continues giving birth. Keep a supply of puppy formula on hand for emergency feedings or later weaning. An alternative formula of evaporated milk, corn syrup, and a little water with egg yolk can be warmed and fed if necessary. A pet nurser kit is also a good thing to have on hand; these are available at local pet shops. A supplementary feeding often helps weak pups (those that may have difficulty nursing) over the hump. Keep track of birth weights and weekly readings thereafter; this will furnish an accurate record of the pups' growth and health, and the information will be valuable to your veterinarian.

RAISING THE PUPPIES

After all the puppies have been born, take the mother outside for a walk and drink of water, and then return her to take care of her brood. She will probably not want to stay away for more than a minute or two for the first few weeks. Be sure to keep water available at all times and feed her milk or broth frequently, as she needs nourishment to produce milk. Encourage her to eat, with her favorite foods, until she seeks them of her own accord. She will soon develop a ravenous appetite and should have at least two large meals a day, with dry food available in addition. Your veterinarian can guide you on the finer points of nutrition as they apply to nursing dams.

Prepare a warm place to put the puppies after they are born to keep them dry and to help them to a good start in life. An electric heating pad, heat lamp or hot water bottle covered with flannel can be placed in the bottom of a cardboard box and near the mother so that she can see her puppies. She will usually allow you to help her care for the youngsters, but don't take them out of her sight. Let her handle things if your interference seems to make her nervous.

Be sure that all the puppies are getting enough to eat. If the mother sits or stands instead of lying still to nurse, the probable

While in the womb, each pup is encased in an individual protective sac.

cause is scratching from the puppies' nails. You can remedy this by clipping them, as you would the bitch's, with a pet nail clipper. Manicure scissors also do for these tiny claws. Some breeders advise disposing of the smaller or weaker pups in a large litter, as the mother has trouble handling more than six or seven. You can help her out by preparing an extra puppy box or basket furnished with a heating pad and/or heating lamp and some bedding material. Leave half the litter with the mother and the other half in the extra box, changing off at two-hour intervals at first. Later you may exchange them less frequently, leaving them all together except during the day. Try supplementary feedings, too. As soon as their eyes open, at about two weeks, they will lap from a small dish.

A puppy nurser kit is considered standard equipment by many breeders. These kits are available at your local pet shop.

WEANING THE PUPPIES

Normally the puppies should be completely weaned at five weeks, although you can start to feed them at three weeks. They will find it easier to lap semi-solid food than to drink milk at first, so mix baby cereal with whole or evaporated milk, warmed to body temperature, and offer it to the puppies in a saucer. Until they learn to lap it, it is best to feed one or two at a time because they are more likely to walk into it than to eat it. Hold the saucer at

their chin level, and let them gather around, keeping paws off the dish. Cleaning with a damp sponge afterward prevents most of the cereal from sticking to the pups if the mother doesn't clean them up. Once they have gotten the idea, broth or babies' meat soup may be alternated with milk, and you can start them on finely chopped meat. At about four weeks, they will eat four meals a day and soon do without their mother entirely. Start them on canned dog food, or leave dry puppy food with them in a dish for self-feeding. Don't leave the water dish with them all the time; at this age everything is a play toy and they will use it as a wading pool. They can drink all they need if it is offered several times a day, after meals. As the puppies grow up, the mother will go into their "pen" only to nurse them, first sitting up and then standing. To dry up her milk supply completely, keep the mother away for longer periods; after a few days of part-time nursing she can stay away for even longer periods, and then permanently. The little milk left will be resorbed by her body.

The puppies may be put outside during the day, unless it is too cold or rainy, as soon as their eyes are open. They will benefit from the sunlight. A rubber mat or newspapers underneath will protect them from cold or dampness. As they mature, the pups can be let out for longer intervals, although you must provide them with a shelter at night or in bad weather. By now, cleaning up after the matured youngsters is a man-sized job, so put them out at least during the day and make your task easier. If you enclose them in a run or kennel, remember to clean it *daily*, as various parasites and other infectious organisms may be lurking if the quarters are kept dirty.

You can expect the pups to need at least one worming before they are ready to go to new homes. Before the pups are three weeks old, take a stool sample from each to your veterinarian. The vet can determine, by analyzing the stool, if any of the pups have worms—and if so, what kind of worms are present. If one puppy is infected, then all should be wormed as a preventive measure. Follow the veterinarian's advice; this also applies to vaccinations. You will want to vaccinate the pups at the earliest possible age. This way, the pups destined for new homes will be protected against some of the more debilitating canine diseases.

THE DECISION TO SPAY OR NEUTER

If you decide not to use your male or female for breeding, or if you are obligated to have the animal altered based on an agreement made between you and the seller, make the necessary arrangements with your veterinarian as soon as possible. The surgery involved for both males and females is relatively simple and painless: males will be castrated and females will have their ovaries and uterus removed. In both

REASONS TO SPAY/NEUTER DOGS

- Reduces dog's need to roam.
- Reduces and/or eliminates certain reproductive cancers.
- Disburdens female dog of heat cycle and discomforts which accompany.
- Lessens dominance and mounting activity.
- Increases general lifespan of dog.
- Eliminates owner's concern of unwanted puppies, runaway stud dogs, stained furniture, nervous, and aggressive mood swings in pets.
- Relieves community of homeless dogs and property damage.

cases, the operation does not alter their personalities; you will, however, notice that males will be less likely to roam, to get into fights with other male dogs, and to mount objects and people.

Your veterinarian can best determine at what age neutering or spaying should be done. With a young female dog, the operation may be somewhat more involved, and as a result be more costly; however, in the long run you will be glad you made the decision to have this done for your pet. After a night or two at the veterinarian's or an animal hospital, your bitch can be safely returned to your home. Her stitches will heal in a short time, and when they are removed, you will hardly notice her souvenir scar of the routine operation. Once she has been spayed, she no longer will be capable of

having a litter of puppies.

Check with your city or town or with the local humane society for special programs that are available for pet owners. In many municipalities you can have your pet altered for just a small fee; the low price is meant to encourage pet owners to take advantage of this important means of birth control for their dogs. Pet adoption agencies and other animal welfare organizations can house only so many animals at one time, given the money, space, and other resources they have available. This is why pet owners are urged to have their pets altered, so that puppies resulting from accidental breedings won't end up being put to sleep as so many others have that are lost, stray, unwanted, or abandoned.

Traveling With Your Pet

Most pets can be trained to become very good travellers provided you begin that training when your pet is still very young. Unfortunately, your puppy's first ride in the car is likely to be to the veterinarian's where, after a frightening, abrupt introduction to the noisy, jolting automobile, he is stabbed by horrible long needles. Is there any wonder that, in the future, he will run for cover whenever he hears you jingling your car keys?

TRIPS BY CAR

Familiarize your pet with your car by taking him to a nearby park or an open area where he can run about and enjoy himself. Thus, you will have associated the car with something pleasant. Throw a dog biscuit or favorite toy into his crate, which you have placed on the back seat of the car, in an effort to preoccupy him. Never allow your dog to ride uncrated, as there is nothing more dangerous than a playful pup jumping on his owner as he is driving. Your puppy should also keep his head inside a moving car as dust and debris could irritate his eyes and nostrils.

When you park your car and leave your pet inside, make certain that the windows are open at least two inches; dogs are particularly susceptible to heat exhaustion and the temperature in a parked car in the height of summer can reach over 120°F. Try to find a shady spot to park your car and return as soon as possible, as unscrupulous dognappers do exist who might pounce on your unsupervised pet. Of course, you must NEVER put your pet in the trunk of your car.

LONG TRIPS

When you prepare for a lengthy trip, make certain that you pack a few essential items for your canine companion: a blanket, a thermos of water, pet food, his food and water dishes, favorite toys, and any necessary medicine.

Do not give your pet a heavy meal before the trip but do ensure that he has a plentiful water supply. This will mean that you will have to break your journey several times so that he can relieve himself, but the rests and exercise will probably do you both good.

Most hotel chains in the United States welcome well-behaved pets but it is always wise to ask about their policy ahead of time when you make your reservation.

With early training and a little common sense, you and your pet will make excellent travelling companions *and* benefit from each other's company along the way.

BOARDING YOUR DOG

It may be necessary one day, however, to board your dog while you are on an extended vacation or business trip. In the United States, kennels which are members of the American Boarding Kennels Association should provide very good care for your pet. The A.B.K.A. is a nationwide non-profit organization established to promote high standards and professionalism in the pet-boarding industry.

Make certain to visit the kennels for an inspection before you board your dog. Examine the facilities, check the cleanliness of the stalls and exercise runs, talk to the owners about any special dietary or medical requirements your dog may have, look at the dogs staying there, and find out if there is a veterinarian on call. Also make your reservation well in advance, particularly if you plan to be away in the busy summer months or during the sometimes hectic holidays.

You can help your pet feel less homesick by taking his bed or favorite toy along. Finally, remember to leave an address or telephone number where you can be reached in case of an emergency.

Always include the dog's favorite toys in his crate whenever you travel by car.

Dog Books from t.f.h.

H-1016, 224 pp
135 photos

H-969, 224 pp
62 color photos

H-1061, 608 pp
Black/white photos

TS-101, 192 p
Over 100 pho

TW-102, 256 pp
Over 200 color

TW-113, 256 pp
200 color photos

H-962, 255 pp
Nearly 100 photos

SK-044, 64 pp
Over 50 color
photos

PS-872, 240 pp
178 color illustrations

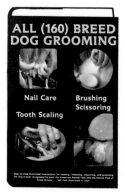

H-1095, 272 pp
Over 160 color illustrations

All-Breed Dog Books From T.F.H.

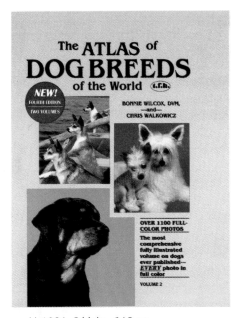

H-1091, 2 Vols., 912 pp
Over 1100 color photos

H-1106, 544 pp
Over 400 color photos

TS-175, 896 pp
Over 1300 color photos

The T.F.H. all-breed dog books are the most comprehensive and colorful of all dogs books available. The most famous of these recent publications, *The Atlas of Dog Breeds of the World,* written by Dr. Bonnie Wilcox and Chris Walkowicz, is now available as a two-volume set. Now in its fourth edition, the *Atlas* remains one of the most sought-after gift books and reference works in the dog world.

A very successful spinoff of the *Atlas* is *The Mini-Atlas of Dog Breeds,* written by Andrew De Prisco and James B. Johnson. This compact but comprehensive book has been praised and recommended by most national dog publications for its utility and reader-friendliness. The true field guide for dog lovers.

Canine Lexicon by the authors of the *Mini-Atlas* is an up-to-date encyclopedic dictionary for the dog person. It is the most complete single volume on the dog ever published covering more breeds than any other book as well as other relevant topics, including health, showing, training, breeding, anatomy, veterinary terms, and much more. No dog book before has ever offered this many stunning color photographs of all breeds, dog sports, and topics (over 1300 in full color).

221

Index